A GUIDE TO
ST. SYMEON THE NEW THEOLOGIAN

Cascade Companions

The Christian theological tradition provides an embarrassment of riches: from Scripture to modern scholarship, we are blessed with a vast and complex theological inheritance. And yet this feast of traditional riches is too frequently inaccessible to the general reader.

The Cascade Companions series addresses the challenge by publishing books that combine academic rigor with broad appeal and readability. They aim to introduce nonspecialist readers to that vital storehouse of authors, documents, themes, histories, arguments, and movements that comprise this heritage with brief yet compelling volumes.

TITLES IN THIS SERIES:

Reading Paul by Michael J. Gorman
Theology and Culture by D. Stephen Long
Creationism and the Conflict over Evolution by Tatha Wiley
Justpeace Ethics by Jarem T. Sawatsky
Reading Bonhoeffer by Geffrey B. Kelly
Christianity and Politics in America by C. C. Pecknold
Philippians in Context by Joseph H. Hellerman
Reading Revelation Responsibly by Michael J. Gorman

FORTHCOMING TITLES:

The Rule of Faith by Everett Ferguson

A Guide to
St. Symeon the New Theologian

Hannah Hunt

CASCADE *Books* · Eugene, Oregon

A GUIDE TO ST. SYMEON THE NEW THEOLOGIAN

Cascade Companions

Cascade Books
An Imprint of Wipf and Stock Publishers
199 W. 8th Ave., Suite 3
Eugene, OR 97401

www.wipfandstock.com

ISBN 13: 978-1-62564-116-8

Cataloging-in-Publication data:

Hunt, Hannah

    A guide to St. Symeon the New Theologian / Hannah Hunt

    Cascade Companions

    xx + 130 p. ; 20.5 cm. Includes bibliographical references and index.

    ISBN 13: 978-1-62564-116-8

    1. Symeon, the New Theologian, Saint, 949–1022. 2. Orthodox Eastern Church. I. Series. II. Title.

BX395.S9 H86 2015

Manufactured in the U.S.A.

For Elizabeth and Jon Dixon

Table of Contents

Preface

This book aims to introduce the life, times, and teachings of St. Symeon the New Theologian to modern readers, whether they are of a religious persuasion or not, in an accessible and engaging manner. I have been enthused by Symeon since I commenced postgraduate studies in theology, and focused on his works in both my MA and PhD dissertation. Although he lived over a millennium ago, Symeon's insights offer much to the modern reader, and many of the controversies surrounding his life and witness are very much alive today, as I have discovered in preparing for recent and forthcoming academic visits to Russia. It is hoped that the book will appeal to those who previously knew nothing about Byzantine monasticism, that it will whet their appetite for more, and that the glories of the earlier Eastern Christian tradition absorbed by Symeon will shine through. The freshness and originality of his style and the rigor of his asceticism are a compelling combination. Although he wrote for monks, his works speak to lay people too, and he is a vibrant witness to his period as well as a spiritual inspiration.

This book is dedicated to my parents, who have always supported my academic activities and to whom I owe thanks for the privilege of educational opportunities. To the many great scholars and translators of Symeon with whom I have discussed him over the years, I also acknowl-edge many debts. Thanks are especially due to John Mc-Guckin, John Behr, Metropolitan Hilarion Alfeyev, Dirk Kraüsmuller, Mary Cunningham and Daniel Griggs. For the serious scholar, the bibliography at the end of the book will indicate some more substantial reading on the subject by the scholars named above and other authors. Words in italics denote entries in the glossary. Any errors are en-tirely my own responsibility.

Introduction

"Mystic of Fire and Light," "the brother-loving poor man," "the New Theologian": these varied titles for our subject, an abbot in Constantinople at the turn of the first millennium, reveal part of the story of St. Symeon the New Theologian. They suggest the many dimensions of a complex and controversial figure whose teachings continue to resonate in the Eastern Christian (Orthodox) world today. For the sake of clarity, St. Symeon the New Theologian will be referred to throughout as Symeon and St. Symeon Eulabes (also known as Symeon the Studite) as Eulabes. As a young man Symeon held office in the *Byzantine* court before becoming a monk and not long afterwards an abbot. He inspired and then infuriated his monks such that a number of them rebelled and left his monastery. Later he was exiled for reasons that straddle the political and the theological; some of his pupils followed him into exile and one of them, decades after his death, wrote a glowing testimonial to his life and works. Today he is revered by the Eastern Christian (Orthodox) church as a saint, as a writer of intensely personal mystical poetry, and as a key exponent of the tradition of spiritual fatherhood, itself a contentious topic in today's world. This book will outline Symeon's life, work, and thought and place him in his religious, political, and social context as a key figure within the

Byzantine church, a place of intrigue and ambition where the authority of the emperor jostled against the authority of the established church and the more individualistic insights of monks who experienced mystical encounters with God. It will introduce the range and scope of his extraordinary writings and consider the impact he had on subsequent generations of Eastern (Orthodox) Christians through the inclusion of his texts in *The Philokalia* and his significance for scholars of the period and of the church he represented. Chapter 1 will outline the historical context for Symeon. Chapter 2 will explain why we need to employ some skepticism in reading medieval sources, and also set out the different types of writing that Symeon used to explain his theological insights. Chapter 3 focuses on Byzantine monastic life and the concept of spiritual fatherhood which was transmitted from one spiritual "father" to his spiritual "son," who in turn became a spiritual "father" to the next generation of novices. Chapters 4 and 5 analyze key areas of his thought and chapter 6 assesses the impact Symeon has made on Eastern Christianity and beyond.

Symeon's dates are generally agreed to be 949–1022 and his lifespan coincided almost exactly with that of Emperor Basil II, who represented the culmination of the Macedonian dynasty. Recent studies of his life have focused on his theology, but it is also advantageous to place him within the political and historical context of his day.[1] Basil's accession to the imperial throne was associated with the relatively common phenomenon of court intrigue. There was no clear accession process and Byzantine history records many political skirmishes, palace intrigues, and possible assassinations, as different interest groups vied to place their contender on the throne. At the turn of the millennium, the Byzantine political scene was shaped by

1. Golitzin, *Mystical* (vol. 3), 7–173.

a handful of very successful and powerful extended families, rather than by any modern type of democracy. Their ability to dominate decision making was enhanced when a putative emperor was a juvenile, as was the case with Basil II, whose reign even once he attained maturity was marked by political factions, violent unrest at court, and potential curbs to his foreign as well as domestic policy. An ambitious and austere figure, Basil remained unmarried all his life, which was extremely unusual for emperors. He spearheaded the expansion of the Byzantine Empire into the Balkans, and this aspect of his reign gave rise later to the nickname "Basil the Bulgar-slayer." He is reputed to have blinded 99 out of 100 of the Bulgarian captives he acquired in his campaigns, leaving one sighted prisoner to lead the others on their shameful journey home. So focused was he on the need to expand his empire that he took the extremely unusual step of offering his sister Anna in marriage to someone who was not at the time a baptized Christian. Needing military support during one period of civil war, Basil invited the collaboration of Vladimir of Kiev. On his baptism around the time of his wedding, Vladimir took on the name of Basil in honor of the emperor, and the mass baptisms which followed helped consolidate the conversion of the Kievan Rus (what we might now know as Russia) at the turn of the millennium.[2]

Basil's strenuous efforts to expand his imperial grasp did not take place in isolation from what we would now call domestic policy; indeed his foreign policy reflected the need to establish and maintain a secure internal situation. Constantinople (or Byzantium as it became known; it is modern day Istanbul) had for over six hundred years been the home of the emperor. Its institution by Emperor Constantine in 320s as the "New Rome" articulated the city's

2. Treadgold, *History*, 498–533.

dual role as the home of secular authority (in the person of the divinely ordained emperor, supported by an immensely complicated and sophisticated civil service) and the religious heart of the Christian Empire in the East. The emperor's status reflected these functions fully. The Christian emperor in the Byzantine world was seen as God's emissary on earth; the order maintained by the highly structured imperial court mimicked the heavenly household or *economia* ruled by God in heaven. The emperor was anointed and crowned in a religious ceremony at the start of his reign. Thereafter, every day started with prayers at one of the city's many churches and court ceremonial merged religious rituals with worldly displays of extravagance designed to show the semi-divine status and power of the emperor. His specific role in these ceremonies is spelled out in a ninth-century Byzantine text, the *De Ceremoniis*, which describes how the emperor performs some functions very similar to those carried out by the higher ranks of clergy in Constantinople. Byzantine culture held close to tradition so the ceremonies delineated in the *De Ceremoniis* were still in place at the time of Basil. The close connection between emperor and *patriarch* was demonstrated by the fact that the emperor alone was permitted to kiss the prelate on the cheek rather than the hand. He was also allowed in the Sanctuary, and even to kiss the altar cloth, as a priest would, something not permitted to lay people. Great splendor and artifice were employed to ensure the Byzantine citizens were impressed by the image of the emperor. Mechanical birds sang at his approach and engineers ensured that gilded lions roared a welcome to him as he processed.

The relationship between the imperial court and the established church was to a degree symbiotic; the bishop anointed the emperor, who in turn selected the bishops for the cities in his empire, and approved appointments within the established church. Although the emperor was conceived of as a semi-divine person, there was, in theory, a separation of responsibility and authority between church and state. The theories for Byzantine statesmanship were taken from ancient tradition, laid down by the church fathers and political theorists. But the two were also interdependent. The city and provincial churches were places of worship and Christian witness for lay people; they were led by priests and bishops who had been appointed by the emperor. The bishops of major cities, known as *Metropolitans*, were especially powerful, as they held positions of responsibility on the *synod* or governing body of the church, which also included members of the Civil Service, in itself a complicated entity. There was therefore a degree of codependency between the court and the church.

The relationship between the court, the church, and the monasteries was more complicated. Monasteries had a less conforming and malleable structure than the "secular churches," which served the laity in the empire. They acted as a powerhouse of spiritual endeavor and prayer for the community. Within each monastery one or more churches provided a space for daily worship by the monks. Constantinople at this time had hundreds of monasteries, some founded centuries previously. They ranged from the famous and highly influential—such as that at Stoudios, where Symeon undertook his early formation—to the small and more maverick. Unlike in the West, the norm was for relatively independent organizations, rather than a monastery being one of many houses of a named order, all of which followed the same rule, as was beginning to happen in the Benedictine order at this time. That said, they did operate according to laid down rules, and as a new monastery came into being its rule or *typikon* normally incorporated insights and practices from existing monasteries. Men withdrew to a monastery, frequently after a lifetime of public service in the military or imperial administration. They provided a space where God could be worshipped without the distracting claims of secular life, family, and professional demands. They demanded a commitment to a life of austerity and obedience, of prayer and contemplation. But monasteries were by no means fully independent of the world, nor could the world neglect its ties to the monasteries. A nexus of financial connections comprising trade, taxes, and tax exemptions and other revenue sources, linked the court and the monastery, requiring co-operation and mutual understanding.

Other factors contributed to the somewhat uneasy relationship between monasteries and the church. Church governance was controlled by ordained clerics, who interpreted the church's doctrine in accordance with the canons of the *Ecumenical Councils* that had been convened by emperors and attended by clergy and monks. The Ecumenical Councils forged consensus over matters of faith and practice, but in so doing also established and articulated schisms within the church, with those who failed to conform being *anathematized*. The *synod* would provide the framework for local interpretation of some ecclesiastical matters. There was considerable local variation as to quite how these tenets were interpreted; for example, in the fourth century, the prominent priest Arius of Alexandria asserted a different understanding of the person of Jesus to the one that became deemed the correct orthodox understanding. He was condemned by Ecumenical Councils but not before he had held, for some time, a position of considerable respect in a prominent church in Constantinople, and he attracted a sufficiently large following that it took more than one church council to condemn him and discredit his teachings. Similarly Nestorius of Constantinople, a monk from Antioch, was condemned by the Council of Ephesus in 431 for a divergent understanding of how the divinity and humanity in Jesus Christ were united. Yet to this day many of the smaller Eastern Christian churches see merit in his teachings, and they would be insulted to be termed heretical "Nestorians." Some of the most contentious debates in the Ecumenical Councils took place where monks, predominantly those from Egypt, refused to accept the rulings of clerics. This history of friction between monks and the so-called "secular" church may have underpinned some of the issues experienced by Symeon in the early eleventh century, as it represents a power struggle between the officially sanctioned authority of the emperor and church and what Symeon saw as a more subjective, mystical authority found in some monks.

By the turn of the millennium in geographical, cultural, and religious ways Constantinople occupied a pivotal place between the East and the West, having a foot in both Europe and Asia Minor. The Christian church had been divided by religious schism for centuries and while Antioch and Alexandria were significant centres of slightly divergent ways of approaching Christian thought (in particular how they understood the *dual natures of Christ*), Constantinople had also provided a number of key figures in the theological debates. Its suburb and summer outpost, Chalcedon, had been the location for the formative Ecumenical Church Council in 451. As a trading centre, Constantinople offered opportunities to Venice and other parts of Italy, Arab neighbors, Russia, and others. As a metropolitan centre it contained a diverse range of ethnicities and cultures, as demonstrated by the languages in which surviving written sources were composed. A sophisticated and complex culture, it was informed by diverse currents of thought and experience.

Two key contemporary texts survive giving accounts of Emperor Basil II's life, the *Chronographia* of the great humanist Michael Psellos and John Skylitzes' "summary" of Byzantine history.[3] Byzantine historians believed that rhetorical embellishment of the "facts" they were recording was an essential skill so these sources need to be read cautiously as they do not resemble the more objectively constructed historical approach of today. They were deliberately selective in the facts they recorded and the writers took pride in producing exciting, readable accounts that responded to political expediency. Where the writers were associated with the court they may well have felt obliged to present their subjects in a particular way. Basil is portrayed as an ambitious and determined statesman who after waiting in the wings for many years took office and used the Civil Service administration at his disposal to expand his empire and reform the legal and tax arrangements that threatened to allow powerful aristocratic families to hold too much power. At a certain point in his life he appeared to become more pious, and there was much speculation as to the reasons for this. Some people suggest he may not have married because he wanted to avoid interference from a wife's family, having suffered from much frustration of his aims during his minority at the hands of an uncle, Basil the *Parakoimomenos*. His prowess on the battlefield was legendary, and is contrasted by Psellos with his younger brother's frivolous preference for hunting and feasting.

In addition to written sources there are also nonverbal sources—such as silk fabrics, seals, coins, and other material images, which, like textual sources, are open to interpretation. As we will discover in chapter 2, the genre

3. Sewter, *Psellos,* 27–52, and Wortley, *Skylitzes,* 245–348.

of a source must be appreciated in order to understand how reliable it is as a witness to our subjects' lives. Was the text intended as a straightforward historical account, or was there some political or spiritual bias? Who was recording the events, and for what audience? The issue of genre is especially pertinent with Symeon, much of whose life story is recorded either by himself or by one of his devoted pupils, inspired to record his master's life a considerable time after his death.

ONE

Historical Context to
St. Symeon the New Theologian

Sources for Symeon's Life

Written evidence for Symeon's life and times derive from two key sources, neither of them very objective to modern eyes. The first is a biography or *vita* by his pupil and disciple Nicetas Stethatos. The obvious problem with an account by someone's own pupil, especially in a religious context, is that it is likely to be *hagiographic*, in other words it will overemphasize the holiness and virtue of its subject. This can be done by manipulating the facts, omitting or overemphasizing some, to create a particular picture of the revered person. Stethatos, who ended up as Abbot of the Stoudios Monastery, claimed that towards the end of Symeon's life the old man effectively appointed him as his literary heir. Just as the younger Symeon had a vision of his spiritual father, Eulabes, so in turn Symeon's pupil had a vision of his mentor; thirteen years after he had died

Symeon appeared to Nicetas in a dream, requesting that he write the story of his life and publish his writings.

In addition to the biography, there is also a great deal of evidence about his life smuggled into his own writings, where he sometimes uses the pseudonym, "George" (which may have been his baptismal name) as a disingenuous attempt to disguise his identity. Not much is known about Symeon's early life. He was born in Paphlagonia, an area of Asia Minor between Galatia and the Black Sea, probably around 949 CE. His family was aristocratic, and being ambitious for a courtly career for their son it is possible the lad was castrated, as some court positions were only available to eunuchs. The status of eunuchs (and whether or not Symeon became one) is contentious within the church and debated by historians: in part, it was presumed that being unable to father children, a eunuch would remain loyal to his employer. At the age of eleven, he was removed from the family home and sent to the court under the protection of his uncle.

The young man apparently progressed within the Byzantine civil service, experiencing an abrupt interruption to the family patronage, which had placed him in court when his uncle was murdered during the civil war in 963. It is barely possible to separate the demise of his political career from the emergence of his enthusiasm for the religious life. For well born men in the Byzantine court the monastery was already a place of refuge, refreshment, and advice; having the right spiritual father added to your social standing, and even those people who took public office might, when they felt the need, consult with an advisor in a monastery. Such a practice is still common for modern Orthodox Christians—and can cause controversy as we shall see in chapter 6. For centuries there had been a sense in Byzantine society that monasteries were a spiritual powerhouse, and that having a saint or holy man in your town or village was a benefit to everyone. So it was not unusual that Symeon went occasionally to a local monastery for counsel. He started to visit the Studite monastery in the capital on an occasional basis. In his *Discourse 22* Symeon describes how "George," who lived in the city of Constantinople and led a normal worldly existence, encountered a monk who started to guide him towards spiritual reading appropriate for monastic formation. Symeon records how "One day, as he stood and recited, 'God, have mercy upon me a sinner' . . . suddenly a flood of divine radiance appeared from above and filled all the room." (The prayer Symeon was reciting is known as the Jesus Prayer in the Eastern Christian tradition, and it is widely used today for private devotion.) Like St. Paul on the road to Damascus, Symeon loses awareness of his surroundings and in this ecstatic condition has a vision of light surrounding "the saint of whom we have spoken, the old man equal to angels, who had given him the commandment and the book."[1] This is a pivotal moment for Symeon. This and other visions of divine light are recorded at much greater length in his *Hymn* 25.[2] But what is crucial here is that he sees the monk Eulabes (whose name means "piety" or "the pious one") surrounded by light and he then came to himself and "wept with all his heart, and sweetness accompanied his tears."[3] As we shall see in chapters 4 and 5, penitent but joyful tears and visions of light are ways in which Symeon measures the authenticity of a mystical encounter with God. It is on this basis that he claimed his spiritual father Eulabes was a saint and that even though he was not ordained it was such men who had demonstrably had a direct encounter with

1. De Catanzaro, *Discourses*, 243–46.
2. Griggs, *Divine Eros*, 194–99.
3. De Catanzaro, *Discourses*, 245–46.

God, who had the power to remit sins that were confessed to them.

Important as this encounter was, he did not immediately leave his position in the Imperial court, and in fact the years he spent as an adolescent in the opulent surroundings of the palaces of Constantinople provided him with a treasury of images he later used to contrast the indulgent life of court to the ideal, ascetic life. There are many references in his writings to the splendors of the Byzantine court where he had been a minor official; the light-filled palaces with their rich hangings; the encounters with the emperor that parallel biblical parables; even the purple robes of the imperial family, which are, he reminisces, merely a pale imitation of the divinity of Jesus expressed by the royal purple of his blood shed for all sinners.[4] The emperor's imperial grandeur is nothing compared to the kingship of Jesus Christ. He writes retrospectively of the life he left behind, deriding gluttony, fine clothes, "a surfeit of baths and scents," riding horses, attending banquets, sleeping too much, and the more serious sin of fornication.[5] Increasingly, though, he hungered for light, not of gold and fine glass, but of another dimension, the light of God which shone around Moses and which transfigured Jesus on the mountain. This light signified the presence of God. Very much like St. Augustine of Hippo in the fourth century, Symeon writes retrospectively of his need for a mentor, to rescue him from the temptations of his wayward youth: "I wanted, O Master, to find a mediator and ambassador . . . that through his intercession and my submission to him I might find forgiveness for my many offences."[6]

4. *Second Theological Chapter,* McGuckin, *Symeon,* 64–65, and *Discourse 23,* De Catanzaro, *Discourses,* 257.

5. *Discourse 30,* De Catanzaro, *Discourses,* 319.

6. *Discourse 35,* De Catanzaro, *Discourses,* 361.

Writing retrospectively, as did Augustine, Symeon gives thanks that God gave him the free will to turn his back on his debauched past and that God grabbed him by the hair of his head, dragging him out of the filthy ditch of his wrongdoings. The image of being soiled is continued when he describes how Christ effectively handed him over to Eulabes, in a besmirched condition, still "wholly defiled, with my eyes, my ears, and my mouth still covered with mud." This represented his sensual engagement with the pleasures of the world. In his account, Christ instructs Symeon to "Hold on to this man, cleave to him and follow him, for he will lead you along and wash you."[7] Stethatos' biography describes a number of visionary experiences that consolidated Symeon's conviction that he should become a monk. In 977 the young Symeon took his own possessions and "his personal servants, and whatever he had acquired from other income," mounted his horse, and "galloped wildly away."[8] He entered the Studite monastery where Abbot Peter placed him under the care of Eulabes. For the first year he slept under the steps of the elder's cell.

Early Monastic Formation

It is hard to be certain of all the factors in Symeon's change of direction at this point in his life. Going into the monastery meant leaving his life at the court where he had held a role of some responsibility in the civil service. As a child he had benefitted from the patronage of an uncle who was in the imperial court, and like other adolescents away from home, he enjoyed indulging in the normal dissipations of a comfortably off young man. As suggested above, it is also

7. *Discourse 36*, De Catanzaro, *Discourses*, 370.

8. Greenfield, *Life*, 25.

possible that his move away from the court was due to the death of his uncle in the backlash against aristocracy encouraged by the young emperor, whose advisor during his minority had also not favored aristocrats. Byzantine society at the time was dominated by a handful of very influential and well-connected wealthy families and Basil's unease with this situation can be traced through the legislation he undertook to undermine their power. So political disappointment, or even recognizing the need to keep a low profile, may have contributed towards the young Symeon's change of direction.

Quite how much he was in need of repentance is also hard to determine. It is common for hagiographical accounts to exaggerated juvenile misdemeanors as a conventional way of showing how reformed a character the subject was after conversion. He did appear to embrace his new life with fervor. At the Studite monastery Symeon took instruction from the elder Symeon, who apparently had to reign in the youngster's enthusiasm for ascetic endeavor by suggesting that excessive fasting and keeping of vigils was not necessary. Since obedience to your elders was essential, Symeon would have been guided by this, as in his choice of spiritual reading matter. The "book" he mentions being given to read was a text by Mark the Monk, one of the *Desert Fathers*, which would have been something the elder Symeon had himself been given to read during formation by his "father."[9] After around a year, Symeon's intense devotion to his spiritual father, with whom he shared a cell, caused unease in the monastery, and in 980 he was moved to the smaller monastery of St. Mamas, to the west of the city. According to Stethatos this was in a state of disrepair, a not uncommon state in a city where it was more popular to build a new religious institution than to repair and

9. *Philokalia* (vol. 1), 109–60.

upkeep an existing one. (This was such an issue in general
that Basil II enacted legal measures—known as Novels—to
dissuade wealthy patrons from adding to the problem.)

Symeon as Abbot of St. Mamas

Once ensconced at St. Mamas, Symeon experienced rapid
advancement. Within a short period of time he had been
tonsured as a monk and shortly afterwards ordained as
a priest. It is hard to tell quite when he took on various
types of responsibility within the monastery but it is fair
to say he was still a young man when, on the abbot's death,
he was elected as the new abbot, around 980. This took
place within three years of his arrival. From Symeon's own
writings and the hagiographical accounts given by Nicetas
it is evident he worked strenuously to improve both the
material and immaterial aspects of the monastery to which
he moved. St. Mamas was the patron saint of Symeon's
birthplace, so he may have been able to make connections
with other men from his home area to assist his career at
this point. As he legitimately brought with him his private
wealth and the monastery was very dilapidated he was able
to contribute to its refurbishment. The physical dilapida-
tion of the monastic buildings was matched by neglect
in the moral condition of the community. His elevation
to authority seemed to outstrip his experience in han-
dling people; his fervor to reform (another conventional
enthusiasm often attributed to eminent clergy or abbots)
combined perhaps with an immature ability to handle dis-
putes was to cause a considerable rebellion. The church at
the monastery of St. Mamas contained the tombs of the
sixth-century emperor Maurice and his wife and members
of his household. Symeon's programme for rebuilding St.
Mamas included removing these remains and the laying

of a new floor. It is possible he did this in order to shake off the shackles of imperial patronage for the monastery; whatever the reasons, it is typical of the vexed and complicated relationship between imperial authority and the newly invested power of an abbot.

As well as being in need of physical refurbishment the monastery was spiritually dilapidated. Men had various reasons for entering a monastery; some scholars have debated the extent to which a midlife desire for the religious life was a means of avoiding taxes or military service or simply accommodated a disinclination for family life in a culture where marriage and childrearing was expected of a citizen. Symeon felt that some of the monks lacked real commitment to the ascetic life and were just there as a refuge from other responsibilities. Over the next decade or so, at the same time as physically rebuilding, he made strenuous efforts to improve the ascetic standards of his monks and increase vocations from those as yet outside. His vivid *homilies* written to be delivered verbally to the monks are testimony to his deep-rooted knowledge of Scripture, his recognition of the temptations of the world they had left behind (he refers to the court, to theatres, and to other secular pursuits), and his understanding of their need for the right sort of guidance. They were intended to exhort his monks to make greater efforts in their prayer life and to encourage them to put aside the temptations and old practices associated with their former lives. These *homilies* also insist on the need for tears of repentance, the need for obedience to the spiritual father, and the importance of an almost physical awareness of God's presence within.

Conflict within and outside the Monastery

Symeon was filled with zeal to improve the standards at St. Mamas, but innovation and change are not always welcome and while Symeon may have had the best motives his critique of the establishment he inherited was not always well-received. Around 996–98 about thirty of the monks rebelled against him and stormed out of the monastery. The context of this, and how Symeon responded, tells us quite a bit about his attitudes to his "spiritual children."[10] The uprising took place during his delivery of a sermon after the morning office; if we knew which one (and whether it was one of those that survived and is available to us today) we would know more about what exactly he said that so enraged his flock. From Stethatos' account, his language was uncompromising: on this occasion he was "admonishing, persuading, and exhorting according to the apostle's advice." When in response to this the rebels rushed at him like "barking dogs," he stood quietly "motionless in his place, smiling and gazing radiantly at those vengeful men," who then broke the locks of the monastery gate and ran towards the home of the *patriarch*. This was an act of extreme disloyalty; their spiritual advisors who had authority over them were members of the monastery, and did not belong to the established "secular" church which served the lay people in the city. The *Patriarch* of Constantinople at the time, Sisinnios II, became embroiled in the debate and decided to condemn the rebels to exile. Rather than leaving matters there Symeon appealed against this judgment and finding that the rebels had scattered to the four winds he painstakingly sought each one out, finding them in temporary homes within other monasteries and

10. Greenfield, *Life*, 83–89.

churches. His biographer does not record how successful this attempt at reintegration was.

Further issues with authority had a less happy outcome. Abbots were by no means separated entirely from city life and commercial activity, but the nature of monastic life encouraged a great emphasis on individual visionary encounters with God as the source of authority in spiritual life. This could be at odds with the power imposed from outside the monastery. This was especially so for Symeon, who had been so greatly influenced by his charismatic "father" in God, the Studite monk Eulabes. However, while he did assert the authority of charism, at no point did Symeon suggest that Holy Orders in themselves, or the sacraments which could only be offered by ordained priests, were unnecessary; far from it. But his strident disregard for convention provoked hostility. Symeon's devotion to his spiritual father was one of the causes for more serious friction with the established church, and this came to a head in a disagreement with Stephen of Alexina, the *synkellos* of Basil II. By the time of the conflict with Symeon the New Theologian, Stephen was a much trusted member of the establishment, respected because of his advice on foreign policy during the troubled civil uprisings that plagued Basil's minority. He had previously been the *Metropolitan* Bishop of Nicomedia and had also possibly acted as a spiritual father to a pious military advisor to the court, Nicephorus Ouranos. He therefore had grounds for setting himself up as a theologian. The two men had some things in common. Both had been ordained, had experienced monastic life and served in the Byzantine court. But the ways in which they understood doctrinal issues, and especially where they felt spiritual authority lay, differed widely. Although they had both received molding in monastic discipline, they had radically different understandings of what counted. Beside the Scriptures, and the sacraments of baptism and Eucharist, Symeon valued above all mystical experiences of divine indwelling, shown by dramatic visions of God, floods of penitent tears, and an almost tangible sense that God had entered your soul. According to this outlook only empirical knowledge of God gave you the authority to preach, to teach, to absolve sins. Stephen apparently took a more intellectual approach, favoring the emerging scholastic approach in which technical theological terms are clearly and rationally defined. It is possible that a treatise Stephen wrote, the *Syntagma ad quondam politicum*, was the trigger for the angry debate that ensued.[11] Symeon's extensive and impassioned *Hymn 21* records his outrage that Stephen dared to teach about God without the very esoteric spiritual experience Symeon believed was the only ratification for theological teaching:

> If you have not been enlightened by the Divine Spirit,
> If you have not wept tears painlessly . . .
> And you have not found Christ within you even when unhoped for . . .
> How dare you, you who are yourself all flesh,
> And have not yet become spirit like Paul,
> To speak or to philosophize about the Spirit?[12]

Much of Symeon's most impassioned writing against those who theologize in the absence of direct experience of God seems to date from after this conflict, but Stethatos hints throughout his biography of Symeon that the divergent views of the two men were well established before Symeon's exile.

---

11. Krausmüller, "Religious Instruction," 239–50.

12. Griggs, *Divine Eros,* 147.

Symeon's Trial and Exile

The debate started in 1003 after an encounter in the corridors of the imperial palace, which Symeon must have been visiting on one of the occasional visits all abbots needed to make to conduct business. Stephen appears to have asked Symeon to account for his understanding of the Holy Trinity. Symeon asked for time to make a proper response. His teachings on the Trinity in his *Practical Chapters* may have formed part of his written response. The two men were unable to resolve the matter, with accusations and counter accusations flying around, although for the most part we only have written evidence from Symeon and his far from impartial biographer. After an ecclesiastical trial in 1005 Symeon was dismissed from his position as abbot, though he remained for the time being in the monastery at St. Mamas. As well as the theological dispute on understandings of the Trinity, Stephen of Alexina revived anxieties about the reverence paid to the memory of Symeon Eulabes, which till that point had been unchallenged by the church authorities. There is, in fact, evidence that the metropolitan church had supported the veneration of Eulabes, by providing candles and incense for the ceremony. Here we see a degree of conflict of secular and sacred values. Basil II had worked towards rationalizing and centralizing many aspects of his unwieldy Empire. This policy extended to his domestic policy, too, and Symeon's extreme attachment to his mentor did not entirely conform to the official approach to conferring the status of "saint" as laid down by such texts as the *Menologion,* which Basil had commissioned on the advice of his spiritual advisors.

Stephen's role as *synkellos* to the patriarch gave him the ear of not only the highest ecclesiastical authority of the land but also of the imperial court. Depending whose

perspective we look through we get different understandings of the matter. Symeon's own outrage at scholastic
approaches to theology is evident from his own writing.
Nicetas Stethatos makes a number of other accusations,
accusing the church authorities, and Stephen in particular, of envy, deliberate malice, and even what amounted
to demonic possession—not a sound basis for evaluating
the reality of the situation. He described a striking (but
it has to be said rather implausible) reason for Symeon's
condemnation by the court:

> His defence was read aloud for quite some time
> in the midst of the holy synod, and by the force
> of its ideas, the grandeur of its statement, the
> aptness of its examples, the great vehemence yet
> dignity in the form of its actual wording, and
> the brilliance of its truth, it thundered in the
> minds of those who heard it. Since they were
> unable to undermine the force of Symeon's
> statement with fallacious arguments, they rose
> from their seats, tongue-tied in their speech-
> lessness, and, passing sentence on the just man
> by default, condemned him to banishment.[13]

This is rousing stuff, but does not explain what is meant by
"by default"; if Symeon's argument was so persuasive, why
was he condemned? The *hagiographical* bias of the *Life* is
evident here. Internal evidence from the homilies shows
that Symeon was planning a succession, and he evidently
prepared Arsenios to take his place at St. Mamas.

13. Greenfield, *Life*, 217.

Exile, Later Writings, and Death

Sent into exile in 1009, Symeon attached himself to the derelict monastery of St. Marina in the village of Paloukiton, not far from the capital, but across the Bosphorus from the imperial palace. From here Symeon wrote again to Stephen, who apparently added insult to injury by excavating the vacated cell of the monk to see if he could uncover the "wealth" he assumed had enabled Symeon to honor his father in the lavish way he had been accustomed to. Since Symeon had come from a wealthy family he had, indeed, taken his personal wealth into his monastic life, where it was used for the common purse. Symeon also contacted the new patriarch, Sergios, with an explanation of his actions, at which the synod appeared to have a change of heart and invited him to return to the city. But Symeon embraced his exile as a mark of sharing in the sufferings of Christ, his apostles, and the fathers of the ancient church, who had undergone martyrdom in the cause of their beliefs. The establishment agreed to interfere no more with his commemorations of Eulabes.

His departure from St. Mamas heralded the start of a very productive period of his life. He was supported financially by a wealthy patron or *charistikarion* and enabled to establish a new monastery, once again refurbishing a dilapidated site, and it was here he wrote the set of teachings known as the *Ethical Discourses*, which forms an important adjunct to the sermons he had preached to his monks at St. Mamas. He also completed down the impassioned hymns, in which he elaborates on the need for a spiritual father, the requirement to experience God directly, and the desirability of penitent tears when approaching the altar for communion. Many of the hymns, which are very poetic in form, contain lavish outpourings of imagery and praise, but even the most expressive of them is packed with theological teachings that disclose his own understanding of how the traditions of his church should be transmitted. He died on 22 March 1022, from an attack of dysentery. Nicetas Stethatos, though an ardent pupil of Symeon, expressed a modest reluctance to proclaim the virtues of his spiritual father, fearing (perhaps naively) that he lacked the skill to accomplish the weighty task. However, he took on the responsibility and his introduction to the hymns of his master exists and is included in the Greek/French edition of his works. It took a further thirty years before Symeon the New Theologian's remains were returned, as relics, to Constantinople, an indication of the extent to which he had unsettled the authorities who were empowered to make decisions about such matters.

His written legacy was immense in volume and influence; around thirty-six *homilies* written to be read to his monks at St. Mamas; fifteen *Ethical Discourses* written in his seclusion after his exile; three *Theological Discourses* and three sets of *Practical and Theological Chapters* (which take the form of fairly brief collections of sentences along the lines of the *Apophthegmata* of the *Desert Fathers*); and his extraordinarily vivid, daring even, *Hymns of Divine Love*, of which fifty-eight have survived. Chapter 6 will explore the reception and significance of this legacy, including the revival of mysticism in the *hesychastic* movement of the fourteen century as well as the inclusion of his texts (and those of Mark the Hermit, Symeon Eulabes, and Nicetas Stethatos) in the *Philokalia*. It will also explore the contentious nature of the title "New Theologian," which on the face of it seems to go against the experiential basis for authority that Symeon insisted on, since in the orthodox Byzantine world a "theologian" was a speculative thinker (perhaps such as Stephen of Alexina) who was able to separate the religious teaching from the process of living it out. Evagrius' comment in his chapter 60 *On Prayer* that "A theologian is one who prays and he who prays is a theologian" is taken by Eastern Christians to denote the indivisibility of practical experience of the divine, from teaching about it.[14] Symeon appears to have accused Stephen of separating the practice and the experience. Today, it is Symeon's more experiential approach that has continued to stimulate discussions about the role of the spiritual father and the relationship of the Orthodox church to the secular state.

Symeon's Theology

For Symeon the direct experience of the Divine Spirit within the human heart transcends human language, and is perceived by the senses more than by any rational or intellectual means. This sense of divine indwelling must be fully recognized by the person who experiences it. Symeon uses a number of striking images of the feminine to explain this. In both the Greek and Syrian religious traditions this is a common method of describing the work of the Holy Spirit or other sacred phenomena. For example, he describes the saints as fulfilling the role of the human breast: "pouring God's righteousness to those who hunger and thirst for it, providing them with the bread which nourishes the powers of heaven."[15] In the *Fourth Ethical Discourse* Symeon talks about Christ himself appearing as "a breast of light, placed in the mouth of their intellect to suckle them."[16] These are clear re-workings of the Pauline

14. Sinkewicz, *Evagrius of Pontus*, 199.

15. *First Ethical Discourse*, Golitzin, *Mystical* (vol. 1), 43.

16. Golitzin, *Mystical* (vol. 1), 20.

idea of spiritual milk being needed for spiritual "infants," suggesting that only when Christians are a little advanced in their spiritual development can they digest the "strong meat" of harder teaching. Writing to the Corinthian church, the Apostle said: "And I, brethren, could not speak to you as to spiritual people but as to carnal, as to babes in Christ. I fed you with milk and not with solid foods; for until now you were not able to receive it" (1 Cor 3:1–2).

Symeon repeatedly shows how you must be vibrantly aware of God's presence within. In his *Tenth Ethical Discourse* he uses the language of movement to demonstrate the mystical light he believes engulfs one who has experienced God directly:

> The one who has Christ take form within himself and is aware of His stirring, which is to say His illuminations, is in no way ignorant of His leaps, that is His gleamings, and sees His formation within himself . . . [Christ] appears in a light which is personal and substantial; in a shape without shape, and a form without form He is seen invisibly and comprehended incomprehensibly.[17]

This text expresses something at the heart of Symeon's theology, his belief that unless you have intuitively experienced God within you—which he describes in graphic terms as a mother feeling her unborn child move within her womb—then you have no authority to forgive sins or to preach or teach any of the church's doctrines.[18] He affirms those who have experienced this very striking, almost visceral, sense of the divine within themselves. By comparison, he criticizes those who have not undergone such an encounter with the living God. Such a person

17. Golitzin, *Mystical* (vol. 1), 169.
18. Ibid.

"remains but flesh and blood. He cannot gain an experience of spiritual glory by means of his reason, just as men who are blind from birth cannot know sunlight by reason alone." It was, he insisted, essential that a man intuitively "puts on the image of Christ over his rational and intellectual nature."[19]

As we have seen, some of his sermons drew on his own experience of the vision of divine light in which he had seen the "angelic" man who had inspired him. Increasingly he insisted that this sort of ecstatic experience and the shedding of tears should be seen as the norm in monastic life—something not all his monks may have been comfortable with and certainly not listed as a requirement within the guidelines of the average monastery of the day. The *homilies* show that his desire for all his monks to understand this and share in these experiences stemmed from his deep love for them and his concern for their spiritual well-being. He described himself as "a brother-loving poor man," one on a level with his monks, while seeking to set them an example to follow.

Another aspect of his theological understanding was that the living saints who have guided you on your spiritual journey are graced by divine illumination and that this gives them spiritual authority. From generation to generation such charismatic people inspire those at the start of their spiritual journey. He invoked the example of Eulabes and the vision of luminosity, urging his brothers to:

> imitate the repentance of David and of the rest of the saints. Display a worthy penitence by means of all sorts of deeds and words, that you may draw on yourselves the grace of the allholy Spirit. For this Spirit, when He descends on you, becomes like a pool of light to you. . . .

19. *First Theological Chapter*, 53, McGuckin, *Symeon*, 46.

> We have known such a man in our own time,
> our holy father the Studite.[20]

Symeon's belief that Eulabes was a living saint was a contentious one, given that the emperor had supported the establishment of a more structured approach to identifying and commemorating saints through the commissioning of a *Menologion*. The function of such a text was more than just a record of pious observation; by listing those deemed worthy of sainthood it showed Basil's control of people's perceptions of who bore spiritual power in his empire. The calendar and its rubric became a benchmark for assessing holiness. Symeon's enthusiasm for the example of his spiritual father increased with Eulabes' death c. 986/7. He instituted a yearly office and feast day to commemorate the man he saw as a saint, wrote a biography of him (which does not survive), and devised a *kontakion*. Although later accused of thus establishing a cult of his spiritual father, this state of affairs was not challenged from outside the monastery until 1009. His long *Letter One (On Confession)* affirms the importance of finding a good spiritual father, someone who would act as "an intercessor, physician, [of souls] and a good counsellor," and who has been demonstrably "filled with the Holy Spirit." More dangerously he insisted also that such a confessor need not be formally ordained by the church and that because "the bishops had become useless" and the priests "polluted," the authority to bind and lose sins had been transferred "to God's elect people, I mean to the monks."[21] In some of his works, this sort of criticism of authority figures seems to be angled towards specific individuals, such as Stephen.

20. *Discourse 32*, De Catanzaro, *Discourses*, 335.
21. Golitzin, *Mystical* (vol. 3), 193–97.

Subsequent chapters will explore the key themes within Symeon's theology in more depth. For now we turn to an examination of the different types of writing used as sources of evidence about the lives of our subjects and how to decode the bias contained within them. We also look at how Symeon's writings communicated his key ideas; the importance of empirical experience in validating the guidance of a spiritual father; the place of tears and visions of light and the means by which the spiritual father's charism was to be observed by the wider church.

TWO

Genres and Styles of Writing

Diversity and Complexity of Byzantine Society

Byzantine society at the turn of the millennium was a rich-
ly diverse culture, in which secular and religious aspects
jostled for supremacy. Successful public figures needed to
understand both the realities of the secular world and the
different demands of the religious life, whether that was
in the bustling city churches or in monasteries set aside
for a more secluded way of life. As noted in the Introduction, the emperor was viewed as a semi-divine personage,
God's regent or representative on earth, who ruled his
empire in imitation of the heavenly kingdom. He had to
be a statesman and soldier, a pious defender of Christian
faith, and a good manager of the resources of the Byzantine Empire. By the end of Basil II's reign the empire
had virtually doubled in size compared to the end of the
eighth century because he had conquered a number of

neighboring states.[1] Leaders of churches and monasteries also needed a wide set of competencies. Symeon drew on spiritual, administrative, and political experience when he became the abbot of an important monastery in the capital city. It was not sufficient to be a theological thinker and writer, or even just a good pastoral leader. Having come from an aristocratic family Symeon well understood the nature of patronage and how he could enable a monastery to run as a successful business, functioning not simply as a prayerful refuge from the demands of political life but also playing a key part in the Byzantine economy. As well as providing a model of how to lead a life devoted to God, the abbot needed to train and educate his novices, and ensure that a right balance was found between the intention to live a simple, non-materialistic life and the pragmatic requirements of running and maintaining a large institution with stewardship of books and art treasures, buildings, and farmland. In his writings we can see evidence of the breadth of experience Symeon had before he left "the world." The multi-faceted nature of these various roles is reflected in the complexity of the sources of information about them, especially the written sources that have survived. There is a degree of ambiguity about the written evidence of this period. It needs careful sifting to ascertain its bias and function as it is always dangerous to accept texts at face value. In terms of the biographical "data" about subjects such as St. Symeon or Emperor Basil II this means we need to consider who was writing, why they were writing, and for what audience. We need to place the genre of writing (history, chronicle, *hagiography*) in its historical, social, and religious context and examine the conventions surrounding these.

1. Treadgold, *History*, 534–82.

When we come to read the texts of Symeon himself again we need to be aware of the background to them, and place them within a long-standing tradition of religious and devotional literature. Symeon's writings are particularly complex because much of what we "know" about his life derives from autobiographical accounts in his sermons and poetry; most of the remaining evidence from a biography written some years after his death by an avid pupil of his, who is keen to emphasize Symeon's holiness and downplay any negatives in his life. So before we move onto looking at the themes contained within Symeon's wonderfully vivid and varied writing we need to clarify some of the genres or types of writing that supply the background to his life and on which he drew when he came to write his own sermons, hymns, and other texts. Subsequent chapters will give examples of how his different writings explored the major themes of his teaching. For now let's explore the context to his work by assessing the different types of writing that were popular in the culture of his day.

Hagiography

As noted in chapter 1, the putative biographies of public figures often contained unmerited praise. Accounts of the lives of kings and emperors were written as chronicles, a version of historical writing that conformed to the expectation that an author would select particular parts of a narrative and embellish it for aesthetic effect. Deliberate omissions also took place on the grounds that some events were not considered sufficiently interesting or relevant to the particular "spin" the writer was aiming at. The author might be in the pay of the court or at least be aware of the effect what he wrote might have on his career. When it came to writing about holy men such as bishops, monks, or hermits, another set of conventions come into play. Here too the actual "facts" of the person's life might not be recorded accurately—because the purpose was to produce an inspiring account which would be morally uplifting to the reader. Accounts of the lives of holy men therefore frequently included what to the modern reader may seem super-human examples of renunciation (according to pious accounts, some of the *Desert Fathers* barely ate at all and slept standing up, or voluntarily confined themselves in barrels). Miracles and healings are included to show the power of the holy man; miracles were an obligatory criterion for establishing canonical sanctity. Frequently the subject's precocious piety is remarked on and another convention was that the man in question was "unlettered"; in other words, had not received a formal education, but was intuitively wise. Stethatos attempted to make this excuse explain why Symeon lost the debate with Stephen of Alexina. However, as an aristocratic youth Symeon would surely have received more education than the average peasant even if he had not received a full formal training in rhetoric; Stethatos has his own reasons for making such a claim. Hagiographic texts might be written by someone who knew their subject well. Symeon knew Eulabes extremely well, and in turn his own pupil Nicetas Stethatos would have lived in close proximity to him and been advised by him on a daily basis. But knowing the subject well did not lend itself to what in the modern day would be seen as an objective perspective. Stethatos' hagiographical *Life of Symeon* refrains from mentioning his debauched life in the court, and is instead full of extraneous expressions of admiration and even accounts of miraculous doings, a redaction that skews the bias, providing "evidence" for later canonization of his subject. Given the long delay before he started writing this biography it seems likely that he was setting Symeon up for canonization just as much as he was providing a record of his life. And this excessive praise is counter-balanced by equally extreme judgments about other people. For example, he persistently demonizes Stephen of Alexina, presenting him as manipulative, malicious, and evil, qualities not necessarily essential to winning a legal battle. We'll look at this in more detail in the final chapter of this book, where we examine Symeon's reputation after his death, and the extent to which this was constructed by Stethatos' *Life* of his master.

Autobiography

To understand the context of Symeon's writings we need first to look at autobiography as a genre. The practice of writing about your early life through the retrospective perspective of adulthood was modelled by Augustine of Hippo, whose *Confessions* (written towards the end of the fourth century) uses graphic accounts of youthful debauchery to show God's intervention in his life and his conversion to a pious and chaste existence. Judging your own adolescent sinfulness through the lens of a mature, more spiritual life was a useful convention to demonstrate to the reader (or auditor) how they, too, could turn their life around (this being the literal meaning of "conversion"). The "saint" who shares his wise insights retrospectively shows that he was a very normal lad who experienced just the same human hungers that the readers of his works themselves might be struggling with. Pointing out how far the saintly subject had travelled from a very impious way of life increased the impact of the story, so sometimes the early misdemeanors are also made much of. In a way it is the reverse of hagiography, although it operates to some extent in the same way, by molding the readers' expectations and presenting a constructed image of the subject.

A Guide to St. Symeon the New Theologian

The language Symeon uses, especially in his *Hymns*, is highly personal—impassioned, even. It seems a long way from the monastic ideal of passionlessness and detachment from the world. He writes with rhetorical emphasis to get his points across in a memorable way. In his *Hymn 24* Symeon refers to committing serious crimes in his youth—murder, pederasty, perjury, and blaspheming. He insists that this is a true account and not "in imagery, not in clever metaphor!"[2] *Discourse 22*, written for his monks at St. Mamas, is more restrained in its account of the adolescence of "George." He tailors his account for a monastic audience, focusing on details that would resonate with their experience in mentioning that: "This young man had not observed long fasts, he had never slept on the ground. He had not worn a hair shirt, nor received the tonsure."[3]

By the time Symeon came to write the autobiographical reminiscences found in the *Hymns* and *Discourses* autobiography as a genre had come to effectively replace the saint's lives in Byzantine society. Symeon had another specific reason for writing in this way. The Studite monastery where he undertook his formation under the guidance of Eulabes ran, like most monasteries, according to its *typikon*. Monastic *typika* often included elements from previous rulebooks, reiterating traditions and practices from earliest monastic institutions. It wasn't felt necessary to be innovative; in fact, tradition was seen as immovable and a key criterion for Orthodoxy. Symeon's approach was rather more individualistic, and while both St. Mamas and St. Marina—the monastery where he was first abbot and the one he set up in exile—did indeed eventually have their own *typika* alongside any written rules, Symeon insisted that some aspects of personal experience provided

2. *Hymn 24*, Griggs, *Divine Eros*, 184–85.
3. *Discourse 22*, De Catanzaro, *Discourses*, 247.

valid criteria for personal formation. St. Mamas did not in fact have a *typikon* until some decades after Symeon died. *Typika* could therefore include advice taken from the experience of demonstrably ascetic masters as well as any formally written down rules. Living in close proximity and complete obedience to a truly enlightened elder was seen as just as important as keeping the written rules and regulations about fasting or prayer life within the monastery; it was your spiritual elder who would determine just how you would interpret the written rules. This is why the transparent holiness of a spiritual father was so crucial; his influence on his spiritual "children" was immense. Symeon's accounts of the conversion of "George" could act as an inspiration for his monks in much the same way that an established rule book might, especially as he portrayed the young man as being saved from his wild excesses through the intercession and guidance of his elder. He describes how Eulabes dragged him out of the mud, how the intercession of a spiritual father can rescue even the most degenerate monk. Writing these accounts as a spiritual father himself sent a clear message to his own monks that they should seek out and obey their own spiritual father. The crucial element of experience rather than theory shaped his theology as well as his monastic practices. Autobiography thus functioned also as exhortation to pupils, in a context where being molded through imitation was the mainstay of formation. It provided them with a role model to follow

Homilies

The most extensive body of work composed by Symeon is the two sets of *homilies* or sermons, comprising the thirty-six *Discourses* he composed for delivery at St. Mamas while he was abbot there and the fifteen so-called *Ethical Discourses* written towards the end of his life while he was living at St. Marina. They are also sometimes translated and referred to as *Catecheses* because they contain teaching, like the catechism of the Roman Catholic Church today. Unlike modern sermons these do not obviously commence with an explanation of a biblical reading. They are crammed full of scriptural reference and citation as well as allusions to earlier church fathers, but their function was less to exegete Scripture than to teach monks (not lay persons) about the religious life. So they include discussions of monastic practices such as fasting, spiritual direction, the need for finding and following a spiritual guide, the need for repentance and tears. It was one of the responsibilities of an abbot to address his monks after the doxology that closed the morning service of *orthros* when the whole community would have been gathered together. Delivering a homily provided the public side of teaching a religious community, which went alongside the individualized guidance given to the novice by his spiritual father in daily private meeting; together these created monastic formation. As they addressed the whole community on particular days they share with St. Paul's epistles a sense of being "occasional" writings which treated particular issues of the day. So the comments in *Discourse 12* about restraining idle talk, or in *Discourse 9* on works of mercy suggest that Symeon was responding to specific problems that had arisen in the monastery from day to day. The *Ethical Discourses* clearly reflect the painful period of controversy surrounding Symeon during the first decade of the eleventh century, though they were probably not written down until his exile across the Bosphorus in the second decade of the eleventh century. These are among the most analytical and polemical of his writings: he makes frequent mention of opponents, who he casts not just as personal enemies but as people who through their spiritual arrogance are a danger to right-minded Christians. Their "ethical" component derives from the mature way in which Symeon writes about Christian virtues, his keen understanding of man made in the image of God and saved by His only Son. The sermons are addressed to "brothers and fathers," acknowledging humbly that he was not the only ordained man in the monastery.

Hymns

Symeon's *Hymns of Divine Love* constitute some of the most eloquent and dramatic of religious poetry. He composed these for the most part after he had left the monastery of St. Mamas. The sense of rejection and alienation from the city where he had spent his formative years comes across vividly. He gives exaggerated description of his own shortcomings before he became a monk and his perceived failings in faith and love after he was tonsured. The style of writing, with lots of vivid imagery and many allusions to the court and the city, lends itself to these themes. Elsewhere Symeon explains why it is necessary to use metaphorical language: "We will require the use of images in order to contemplate the Incarnation of the Word and His ineffable birth from Mary the ever-Virgin, and in order to know truly the mystery of the economy from on high, which was hidden before the ages."[4] The concept of the "Word" of God is itself a metaphor and it is through using human approaches to language that God can be made known to humanity. This was widely understood by theological writers and some of them, such as Symeon and

4. *First Ethical Discourse*, Golitzin, *Mystical* (vol. 1), 31.

John Climacus, are especially imaginative in the scope and range of images they use. As we shall see, throughout his writings Symeon uses a lot of images of female reproduction (conception, pregnancy, birth, suckling) to get across his understanding of how humans develop spiritually. His *Hymns* have some striking examples. *Hymn 50* labels those who are not aware of God's grace within them as being "stillborn children"; he also describes those who are faithless are being as unresponsive as corpses.[5] Other imagery is equally colorful. *Hymn 15* develops the Pauline image of the body of Christ having different "members" of the body represented by individual men and women with different attributes and skills (Rom 12:4–5). In a daring, perhaps even provocative, phrase Symeon suggests that "both my finger and my penis are Christ" because the true Christian feels no shame at being entirely transformed by incorporation into the body of Christ.[6] *Hymn 21* lists a number of animals one should use as models for appropriate and inappropriate behavior: he includes a cat, a mouse, a wolf, a dog, a hare, the donkey carrying Christ, a deer, a fox, and a pig![7] The affluent life he had turned his back on, with its rich secular culture, also provides many imaginative images. *Hymn 1* refers to the fine houses, the "brilliant robes of the many dignities" with jewelled crowns, the flowers and furniture, even "the sofas and the bedding" enjoyed in the imperial palace as examples of lives to be dedicated henceforth to Christ.[8]

Although known as hymns, we don't have any record of how they might have been set to music; rather they are impassioned, poetic, outpourings of faith, hope, righteous

5. Griggs, *Divine Eros,* 354.

6. Ibid., 87.

7. Ibid., 154–55.

8. Ibid., 41.

anger, and grief. They were likely intended to be enjoyed by monks as part of the daily diet of spiritual reading. Their subjects are varied and include theological defence and attacks on his enemies, imagined dialogues between himself and God, prayers, penitential expositions, and ascetic exhortations. Precedents for such verse include *Gregory Nazianzus'* longest poem, *Concerning his own life.* It is possible Symeon may also have encountered the works of the mid-sixth-century Syrian Romanos the Melodist, a composer of *kontakia* and verse homilies, but we have no actual evidence of this. In the Greek originals it is possible to trace at least three different verse structures in Symeon's *Hymns.* He was apparently the first writer of religious poetry to make extensive use of a fifteen-syllable meter more usually employed in political writings.[9] As in other areas of Symeon's life politics and religion were not kept in watertight compartments. The intrigues of the Byzantine court supply much fuel for his imagination in these texts.

Practical and Theological Chapters

Two other genres of writing appear in his corpus. The *Practical Chapters* are, despite their name, very brief gobbets of writing arranged into collections (in the case of Symeon, three separate "chapters"). This style of writing was how the earliest monastic insights were transmitted; the so-called *Desert Fathers*, who inhabited deserts in Syria, Palestine, and Egypt from the second century CE onwards, used this brief form of sentence-like writing to capture teachings about Christian virtues and the challenges faced by those who sought to follow a life withdrawn from secular concerns. They were often gathered

9. Ibid., 17–22.

into "centuries" (one hundred brief texts, often no more than a sentence in length) and many fine examples from the first fourteen centuries are extant in the writings of the *Philokalia*. They were written down many years after the death of the *Desert Fathers*. Those by the sometimes anonymous monks are often witty and very earthy; they feature miraculous stories about animals and contain a lot of "human interest." Symeon takes a more austere approach, and his Chapters also contain certain doctrinal teachings and the importance of moving up the spiritual ladder towards experiencing divine illumination, without which he felt no one should dare to teach about God. Translated in the same volume are his three much longer and densely argued *Theological Discourses,* which would have formed a sound defence of his understanding of the Holy Trinity against the attack made on him by Stephen of Alexina. These three texts focus on very specific doctrinal issues, the first stemming from interpretation of John 14:28, where Jesus says he is going to the Father "for my Father is greater than I." It was the sort of scriptural reference that gave rise to much impassioned debate as the nature of the undivided Trinity depended on particular interpretation of such texts. Orthodox teaching states that the Father, Son, and Spirit are equal and that Jesus' comment should not be interpreted to suggest a subordination of the second person of the Trinity. The *Second Discourse* attacks scholastic theological perspectives like those held by his adversary, Stephen; Symeon accuses such people of attempting to theologize without having experienced God directly as an inner consciousness. The *Third Discourse* is perhaps the most extraordinary mixture of genres, progressing from praise for the unity of the Trinity into a highly poetic florid description of God as light: "The chalice of his precious blood is light. His resurrection is light.

His face is light. His hand, his finger, his mouth, his eyes, all are light. . . . Light is the comforter, the pearl, the seed of mustard, the true vine, the leaven, hope, and faith—all are light."[10] This text must have been uppermost in Maloney's mind when he entitled his study of Symeon "Mystic of Fire and Light." Symeon weaves together theological doctrine, sacramental practice, ascetic discipline, and scriptural references. His lively and imaginative style of composition means his writings can now be appreciated at many levels; for their theological insights, to be sure, but also as spiritually uplifting texts, as a stimulus to meditation, and as inspiration for pastoral direction. But at the time they were written the intended audience was the monks for whose souls he had care. So we look next at the nature of monasticism in tenth/eleventh-century Byzantium and how Symeon internalized and modelled the spiritual parenting he had received from Eulabes.

10. McGuckin, *Symeon,* 139.

THREE

Monastic Life and Spiritual Fatherhood

Biblical Models for Monasticism and Spiritual Fatherhood

The rationale and models for both monasticism and spiritual fatherhood derive from the Bible. Withdrawing from the world, temporarily separating themselves from their people, enabled the leaders of a faith community to focus fully on God and understand what he wanted for and from them. In the Hebrew Scriptures it is when Moses and Elijah go to holy mountains, away from the throng of people, that they stand in the presence of God and receive his insights for the chosen people. Moses encounters the Angel of the Lord in a burning bush on Mount Horeb (Exod 3:1–22); Elijah is providentially fed by ravens while in the wilderness by the Brook Cherith (1 Kgs 17:6). Being in the wilderness —whether it is a rocky arid place, a high mountain, or some other desolate, barren place—enforces a reliance on

God's mercy and a dependence on his provision, rather than any human endeavor, to sustain life. When you are somewhere that cannot readily sustain physical life, you turn to more spiritual sustenance. Christian exegesis of the captivity in Egypt frequently casts slavery as sin from which a spiritual leader will lead you, hence the popularity of the image of a "metaphorical" Moses, from the times of the *Desert Fathers* onwards.

Like the prophet Moses, Jesus withdrew into the wilderness at key points in his life, finding in solitude the chance to "meet" God without the distractions of other people. He is recorded as going away from his disciples on several occasions to pray, to struggle with and overcome temptations, and to seek solace from divine, not human, agency. On these occasions he invoked God as his father and specifically renounced human family ties in favor of a community of those who do the will of God, and in which the "father" is not the birth parent but a metaphorical one. "He who does not leave father and mother and brothers and all that he possesses and take up his cross and follow me is not worthy of me" (Matt 10:37–38; 16:24; 19:29; Luke 14:26–27; Mark 8:34; 10:29). Symeon cites this key passage of the New Testament in his *Discourse 20*, which sets out his thoughts on spiritual guides. Many other passages in his writings mention this, but this text focuses on it exclusively. Elsewhere he explains that even though Christians of his day are not living under the type of persecution that would impose suffering they should seek to mortify their selfish instincts and adopt complete obedience to a one who will lead them in the right way. Just as Jesus called on his father, so the monk should call on "the man whom God shows you" to be your father in God.[1] Because of this the monastic tradition has sometimes been criticized for

1. *Discourse 22*, De Catanzaro, *Discourses*, 232.

preaching against family values; as we will see in chapter 6, this friction between rival claims for "belonging" can cause serious disagreements and misunderstanding. Jesus led a nomadic life with a group of followers selected because they shared his vision of a new way of interpreting God's will; this inner circle of dedicated disciples replaced birth family. New models of community were required; in his last hours as he hung on the cross he asked one of his closest disciples and his mother, Mary, to look after each other, even though they were not related (John 19:26–27). This itinerant, even *mendicant*, lifestyle was very far from the conventional pattern of behavior for young Jewish men at the time and he was criticized for it. Christian monasticism consistently returns to models of obedient discipleship and renunciation of human ties as a means of making more space for God.

The abnegation of self-will and autonomy on the part of the spiritual child that was insisted on may seem strange to a modern reader but this was the foundation of monastic practice. Only in renouncing your own desires, which were likely to focus on the carnal rather than the spiritual, would you be truly open to God's will, and through following that you might become a channel of grace for other people. The spiritual father should himself be humble and spiritually illumined; it was his experience of doing God's will that enabled him to show young monks how to follow suit. If a pupil is invited to share a meal with his spiritual father he should do so as he should be eager to obey everything that is asked of him, but he should take nothing for granted and not presume on any intimacy because of the relationship between them. Symeon points out that even John, the "beloved disciple" who rested his head on Jesus' bosom, was "ordered to call himself an unprofitable

servant along with all the rest" (Luke 17:10).[2] This tallies
with his instructions that you should not seek any special
treatment or favoritism from the abbot. The highest calling
might be that of a hermit, leading a solitary life; if your
spiritual guide advised you to take on this lifestyle you
should do this, trusting in his advice. Such obedience and
re-orientation of will led to great insight and a deep sense
of being full of the Holy Spirit, which would come not like
the mighty wind and fire of Pentecost (Acts 2:2–3) but as
a still small voice or gentle breath of wind (1 Kgs 19:12),
an inner knowledge of God that causes great joy alongside humble, penitential tears. In language reminiscent of
Psalm 82:6, Symeon writes that following a monastic path
in complete unquestioning obedience will make such a
man "a friend of God and a son of the Most High, and,
as far as this is attainable to men, a god."[3] Although this
sounds like a "high" calling, it meant nothing if it was un-
dertaken with any pride or sense of superiority. Humility,
perpetual penitence, and willingness to be tested were at
the heart of the desert experience which was reworked by
each generation of monks.

Foundations of Monasticism in the Byzantine World

In Byzantine monasticism responsibility for the moral
and spiritual development of novices was shared between
the abbot of the monastery and the young man's individual "spiritual father" to whom the abbot delegated specific care for their daily practices. There is some ambiguity
about how this division worked and different monasteries

2. *Discourse 22*, De Catanzaro, *Discourses*, 234.
3. *Discourse 22*, De Catanzaro, *Discourses*, 235–36.

handled the formation of new monks in various ways, depending on the traditions of the monastic house. As mentioned earlier, in Eastern Christianity we do not find the clearly defined monastic "orders" of the West, offering a common model disseminated in multiple locations. The arrangements in the Eastern Christian world were much more *idiorrhythmic*, in other words, each monastic house had its own rule book or *typikon*, which was normally compiled from existing material in the *typika* of similar monasteries and some fresh material. This reflected the huge number and vast diversity of monastic establishments in eleventh-century Byzantium. At the turn of the millennium there were an estimated 7,000 monastic establishments containing around 150,000 monks—and this was from a population of between fifteen million and twenty million inhabitants.[4] Novelty or innovation was frowned upon as antithetical to the concept of tradition (*paradosis*), so when a new monastery was established its governance and administration was determined by a *typikon* that would resemble that of other monasteries while incorporating a particular slant to reflect the patronage or particular needs of the new monastery.

The idea of a monastery may suggest a place of tranquillity set apart from the pressures and demands of the outside world; the very first monk, Antony, in the Egyptian desert stressed that this was essential. However, they could not exist without the infrastructure of commerce that also existed in the secular world. Monasteries needed clear governance, a sound financial footing, and an ability to maintain economic viability; these were achieved in part through working with the established non-monastic churches and the imperial government. From the outset, a monastery was dependent on the good offices of

4. Charanis, "The Monk," 73.

a well–resourced secular patron in conjunction with a religious founder or inspiration; these benefactors would want to see their input reflected in the *typikon*, which might therefore include a hagiographical account of the patron or founder's life as well as his particular insights and intentions for the monastery. The founder's name and life would be commemorated annually with liturgies; his generous endowment of a new foundation would also effectively act as an advertisement of his piety and affluence.

The way in which the foundation documents were interpreted depended on the abbot of the day; an important monastic quality was *discernment*, the wise ability to discriminate between options to work out what was the best way forward in any given situation and what pitfalls needed to be avoided. Both monks and those in authority needed to exercise discernment. It helped them determine what should be their daily practices and attitudes; those in authority used it to ensure that they were not abusing their power or acting through ambition, rather focusing on the wellbeing of those in their care. In his advice to novices Symeon urges them to be sure they are following a shepherd and not a wolf (Matt 7:15; Ezek 34:4) and that they are choosing spiritual health rather than corruption.[5] The popularity of some guides could be a dangerous charism if unaccompanied by humility and discernment.

As well as their primary role to provide a secluded place for contemplation and devotion to God monasteries performed other functions. Not least because of the symbiotic relationships with patrons, they housed, as monks, retired public servants, disgraced minor royalty, and relatives of founders, as well as men devoted more obviously to a life of prayer and contemplation. Some monks had held positions of considerable status and influence in their

5. *Discourse 22*, De Catanzaro, *Discourses*, 235, 237.

public life prior to entering the monastery. They might therefore bring various networks of their own to merge with the expectation that the monastic community was to supply your new "family" once you left your home.

Monasteries as Households or Family Units

The abbot was effectively the "father" of the monastery, responsible for the spiritual "children" in his charge. Byzantine society was highly politicized, with allegiance to extended family the norm, and it often displaced personal friendship or other types of intimacy. This pattern was replicated to some extent within the monastery, where sometimes a number of family members entered the same monastery, or where money from an aristocratic household helped provide resources for a monastery. The clan-like nature of society impacted heavily on the fortunes of Emperor Basil II, whose rule was punctuated by outbreaks of what amounted to civil war between different noble families, all vying for position in the court. This was exacerbated by the absence of a straightforward system for imperial succession. Worldly ambition was fuelled by the desire to establish and maintain a reputation. Although not households in this secular sense, the monasteries with which Symeon was concerned were shaped by these considerations. For example, having the "right" spiritual director was a matter of fashion and prestige; if a well-known and influential member of an elite family living in the city chose one particular monk as his spiritual guide then others might try to follow suit. A popular spiritual elder might have "children" both inside and outside the monastery because of this nexus of family networks. We can see evidence of this in Symeon's *Second Letter,* which is clearly written as advice to laity and may well have been a sort of standard letter designed to be sent to several recipients.[6] Political benefit might arise where bonds forged prior to entering a monastery were strengthened when men joined a monastery where they already had spiritual "brothers." Symeon often mentions friendship and family in his writings, not always in complementary terms! Households were strongly defended (physically as well as metaphorically) and so constituted a private, closed environment where misdeeds and corruption could remain relatively undetected.[7]

Another element in the relationship between monasteries and the secular world was that in entering a monastery a young man or woman permanently cut themselves off from their birth family. This could cause offence and distress; the Studite model encouraged complete separation from your home. Eulabes' *Ascetic Discourse* states that you should "regard solely God and the abbot as your father and mother" from the time you enter the monastery.[8] Symeon's hagiographer gives a brief and pitiful account of the young man's elderly father weeping and begging him not to abandon him in his old age, to which the zealous youth replied that he preferred his heavenly father to his earthly one.[9] There are echoes here of Jesus' response when he is chided for ignoring his mother and siblings; he asserts that his "family" now constitutes those who do the will of God and hunger for righteousness, and not necessarily his birth relatives. Detaching yourself from conventional human ties not only liberated you for a fresh focus

6. Turner, *Epistles*, 17.

7. *Discourse 28*, De Catanzaro, *Discourses*, 299.

8. *Philokalia* (vol. 4), 54.

9. Greenfield, *Life*, 23.

on God but also meant that within community monks acted out of obedience to a common "father" and not as a matter of personal preference and choice of companion. This re-orientation of loyalty strengthened the ethos of a monastery and maintained its tradition, with each successive abbot being molded by his own experience of having relinquished family ties in favor of obedience to his spiritual father.

Monastic Formation in the Byzantine world

The practice of molding novices varied, just as the style of monastic foundation varied. Although personal friendships and favoritism would have been strongly discouraged, the close bond between the novice and his spiritual father was emphasized as crucial to the formation of the monk. Symeon first encountered monasticism at the large and famous monastery of the Stoudios, named for its founder, Theodore the Studite, who placed great emphasis on the individual support given to new entrants to the community by experienced and especially pious monks who were not necessarily ordained as priests. Much of what Symeon writes about the matter is shaped by his early encounter with Studite teaching. The abbot of a Studite monastery was regarded as the "head" of the body, with his experienced elders as the eyes and hands and the monks and novices being the feet, in line with the description of Jesus and his followers in Ephesians 5:23. Monks were expected to be completely obedient to the abbot or whoever he deputed to care for their wellbeing. However, any sense of favoritism or over-familiarity was frowned upon: if a monk needed advice from the abbot he should not visit his cell but ask him in public, at the end of the service in church. Apart from anything else, such a relationship might lead to vanity or overly developed self-esteem on the part of a monk so favored. Particular restrictions applied to being alone with adolescent novices: this was explicitly forbidden in the Studite typikon, and in other areas of the Byzantine world measures were in place to avoid the temptation of pederasty.[10]

Where Symeon (and others) write about the "father" in their religious life it is not always clear if they mean their abbot or the elder to whom the abbot had delegated oversight. Both the father of the monastery and your own spiritual father would be teacher, mediator, and even "ambassador" before God. His prayers on your behalf would be especially powerful.[11] Having grown up in this style of monastery Symeon then replicated it at St. Mamas, where he spent the majority of his active life. The Byzantine church held to the concept of tradition, the passing on of treasured insights from generation to generation. One way of expressing this was the concept of the *golden chain* in which each successive spiritual father was a link connecting him back in time to the apostles and Jesus himself. In time your own pupil might become such a link to the next generation of monks. For Symeon being a link in the golden chain was shown by the elder having received spiritual illumination through a mystical encounter with God. This important status meant that the prayers of your spiritual father were especially efficacious. As a pupil of a charismatic "father" Symeon in turn himself developed into a link in the golden chain.

10. Thomas and Hero, *Foundation* (vol. 1), 78.

11. *Discourse 22*, De Catanzaro, *Discourses*, 246.

The Role and Responsibility of the Abbot

The varied responsibilities of an abbot placed many demands upon him, and it is not uncommon to hear of an abbot begging to be released from the role so that he can return to a life of stillness and contemplation. Given the great importance of the abbot within the monastery, the appointment of a new one caused disruption and distress. Where an abbot died his monks experienced not only grief at the human loss but a sense of disorientation and chaos as the community became rudderless. Even though, as Christians, monks believed that their "father" had gone to rest with the Lord, the intense loyalty felt towards the leader of the community left them feeling utterly bereft. Careful planning helped effect a smooth transmission from one abbot to the next. Because of the total obedience owed to the abbot he potentially wielded considerable power and so it was crucial no one took on the role out of worldly ambition or with the wrong intentions. Symeon's *Discourse 18* was probably written as an aide memoire for his intended successor, a monk called Arsenios, in whose development he had been influential. Entitled "On Worthy and Unworthy Superiors" Symeon makes clear in this homily that he is planning the succession to take place while he is still alive so that he can end his days in tranquillity. He outlines the ideal abbot as being: "free from all ambition, without a trace of bodily pleasure and lust, entirely pure from love of money and remembrance of past wrongs, perfectly gentle and free from anger . . . [and see in yourself] the abundant grace of the Holy Spirit enlightening the interior of your heart."[12]

The abbot should be like a "new Moses." The association of Moses with fire and light are significant: a good

12. *Discourse 18*, De Catanzaro, *Discourses*, 217.

abbot, or in Symeon's view, a good spiritual father, would be personally "illuminated" by their direct encounters with God, and this experience of divine epiphany corroborated their validity as leaders.[13] As well as being a role model through his holiness of life, the abbot had specific responsibilities for his monks. He taught them through homilies and was expected to deliver sermons up to three times a week. He was required by canon law to maintain order within the household, and to deal effectively with any disciplinary matters involving his monks. In terms of running his house, as in any high class "household" there were numerous functionaries, each charged with specific tasks; the titles of the roles are very similar, if not identical, to those found in the Byzantine civil service. The monastic household mirrored the imperial court just as the whole of the earthly household was intended to imitate the heavenly kingdom. The buildings of the churches within the monasteries, their archives, treasures (including icons), robes, relics, bread, wine, cellar, and even farmland all had their keepers.[14] As the head of the community the abbot himself needed to travel on business: Symeon advises that he only leave the monastery once a month to "transact the more urgent business of your flock" and the rest of the time should call on the "various bearers of office" to whom he had delegated authority for specific tasks so he could be free to concentrate on the pastoral and spiritual needs of his flock.[15] Because monasteries enjoyed patronage from secular magnates there was also the possibility of complete outsiders to the monastic way of life becoming involved in their communities. The *charistikarion* was a lay person

13. *Discourse 18*, De Catanzaro, *Discourses*, 217.

14. Hussey, "Byzantine Monasticism," 174–75. *Discourse 18*, De Catanzaro, *Discourses*, 211.

15. *Discourse 18*, De Catanzaro, *Discourses*, 222.

empowered to advise on the management and financial stewardship of the monastery. Such a person, who was usually a wealthy aristocrat, might have the best interests of the monastery at heart and endow it with treasures and upkeep the buildings. Conversely some *charistikaria* were in effect absentee landlords who neglected due maintenance and made extortionate demands on the communities. Basil II enacted legislation to regulate and restrict this practise, which had become problematic during the tenth and early eleventh century. It is thought that Symeon himself held such a role, and he certainly benefitted from the process at St. Marina, where the patronage of the *charistikarion* Christopher Phagouras helped him to restore the deserted ruins and maintain a new monastery in which he could end his days. Phagouras had been a spiritual child of Symeon's and came from his home district of Paphlagonia.

So being an abbot was a tall order. Some of the qualities needed for the task seem to contradict each other. He must be at one and the same time an example of humility, contemplation, and piety and capable of holding his own with court officials, representatives of the emperor, and even trading partners. He needed to be a friend and father figure to all his monks, but without encouraging emotional intimacy. Alongside the abbot was the key figure of the spiritual father, the monk appointed by the abbot to take particular responsibility for a novice's development.

The Concept of Spiritual Fatherhood

The spiritual father was the one person involved in every aspect of your daily life as a young monk. It might be that you already had a spiritual father before you entered the monastery; in any event it was for the abbot to select or approve an appropriate and trusted elder who became the "soul-friend" of groups of novices, helping to advise, guide, and support them.

At a practical level the spiritual father would advise those in his care about the smallest detail of their religious observance; how many prostrations to perform, which psalms to sing during periods of worship, how much sleep to take, and even whether you might take a drink of water.[16] This might sound harsh, but it was the norm, and sometimes the advice would be to make less strenuous efforts, rather than heroic self-abnegation. As we shall see in chapter 5, an essential part of the daily routine was the regular disclosure of thoughts to your spiritual father. This was not necessarily the same as formal confession to an ordained monk, and it is unclear from the evidence available whether the daily disclosure of thoughts was followed by absolution or whether it acted predominantly as a cathartic ritual, which certainly in larger houses was delegated to the spiritual father of particular monks or groups of monks.[17] But the insistence that it took place so frequently is a measure of the intense loyalty required of monks in formation and the trust that they were expected to place in their spiritual father in becoming Christ-like.

Symeon's *Discourse 6* is effectively the *summa* of his teaching about the many benefits of finding the right spiritual father. He starts by reflecting on the tradition of those he sees as living saints, the holy men in the past who have inspired and influenced subsequent generations and who were links in the golden chain. The recorded history of their lives and actions tells you only so much, he reports; the invisible gifts of grace are also important and these are inspirational. He commends the perseverance of St. Antony, who grew in the "wondrous light of [God's]

16. *First Theological Chapters*, McGuckin, *Symeon,* 39.
17. McGuckin, "Monasticism," 617.

countenance" (1 Pet 2:9) as he faithfully renounced the world and its ties. The examples of the *Desert Fathers* Arsenius, Euthymius, and Sabas come next. Through close study of the Scriptures and constant prayer they ground down the hardness of their hearts to become humble and penitent, at once grieving for their sins and rejoicing in their election as sons of God. Symeon's mentor, Eulabes, is especially singled out for having renounced friends, relatives, worldly pleasures, and pains; in achieving this state of passionlessness he showed himself to be truly blessed, such that he "shone like the sun" (Matt 13:43) in the midst of the monastery.[18] The gospel passage cited refers to an explanation given by Jesus about the separation of the wheat and the tares; in the same way, he says, humanity will be divided into those who have failed to satisfy God and whose fate will be the eternal flames of hell, and the righteous ones, who will shine in the heavenly kingdom. God's angels will "harvest" men and women and deal with them as they deserve. Willingness to share in the sufferings of Christ will mean you are finally glorified with him, Symeon says, and this model of Christian obedience and renunciation is what helps create a true spiritual leader, who is a shepherd, guide, and advisor.

Symeon's Experience of Being a Spiritual Child

The quest to find such a father occupied Symeon greatly, and he wrote about it frequently in order to emphasize to his own monks and novices that they should take this practice seriously and learn from his own experience. He explains that just as God ordained the death of his Son in order that all who believe in him all will achieve salvation

18. *Discourse 6*, De Catanzaro, *Discourses*, 123.

(John 3:16–17) so God will provide, for those who search, the right man, "a holy and genuine servant of his, who will guide us to salvation and teach us God's will."[19] His devotion to his spiritual father Eulabes (and the whole experience of being a spiritual child) formed one of the two key influences in Symeon's life, the other being the insights of Scripture. As we saw in chapter 1, his own writings and the biography written by Stethatos rehearse the pivotal moments in his youth when he decided to turn his back on his decadent and sinful life and face the light.

Eulabes had been trained at the Studite monastery in Constantinople, and this was significant in the monastic formation of Symeon as the *typikon* of the Stoudios stated an expectation that all monks make a daily disclosure of thoughts to their spiritual father. This, and the whole area of confession, was a major concern to Symeon and will be explored in more detail in chapter 5. The foundation documents of the Studite monastery spell out what was expected of spiritual fathers and their "children." Monks were only permitted to present themselves for the Eucharist if they were humbled by penitent tears. The young pupils were not to exercise their own opinion about any physical or spiritual matter. Instead they should only act on the advice and prayer of their "lord and father" (presumably the abbot) and furthermore take, unquestioningly, the advice given by those who already have knowledge and insight, the elders of the community. These were not necessarily ordained priests; the crucial quality was their piety of life and their charismatic illumination of soul. In addition to giving advice about basics like eating and sleeping, the elder would choose what, other than Scripture, you should read in order to enhance your understanding of a life of prayer. The writings of Mark the Monk recommended to

19. *Letter* 3, Turner, *Epistles*, 97.

Symeon have remained a valued part of the canon of monastic literature. When Symeon got to know Eulabes he realized that he had found a truly enlightened spirit and Symeon's understanding of spiritual authority is based on this criterion. As noted in chapter 1, his autobiographical, visionary, account of conversion places Eulabes in "a flood of divine radiance" which filled his room while he stood at prayer. This focus on illumination makes a direct connection between Eulables' holiness and the relationship between him and his young pupil; it was Eulabes who had steered his reading and taken charge of his discipline.

Visionary accounts of Eulabes and other experiences of ecstatic intimacy with God are conflated and repeated by Symeon and his biographer in a manner that makes it hard to determine how many different visions he experienced. In a way this does not matter because the content of them, as described by both Symeon and Stethatos, affirm the same message: Eulabes is light-filled and this gives him authority to nourish his pupil's spiritual life; the enlightenment stems from the experience of standing in the presence of God; the attendant angels and prophets sometimes mentioned serve to reinforce the status of the holy man, and confirm even greater authority upon him. This authority transmits to the pupil. So one account of a vision describes Eulabes as shining with "divine glory," which spreads to Symeon the young man as he falls before his elder and clasps his feet. This recalls both the effulgence of Christ in his transfigured state and the healing by touch of the woman with the haemorrhage, who by merely reaching out to the clothes of Jesus acquired from him healing, which spread into her whole being (Mark 5:29).[20] The intensity of Symeon's devotion to Eulabes led the abbot to feel that he should move elsewhere and within a year he

20. *Discourse 16*, De Catanzaro, *Discourses*, 363.

was taken to the monastery of St. Mamas, to the west of the city, where again he advanced rapidly. This was the next stage of his training in becoming a spiritual father himself.

Symeon the New Theologian as a Spiritual Father

Chapter 1 has shown a key example of how seriously Symeon took his responsibility as a spiritual father. In the aftermath of the uprising among his monks, he went with humility and pastoral love to each of them and pleaded with them to return. The metaphor used repeatedly here is that of the shepherd and the flock, and the prodigal son, recalling the parables in Luke 15:3–7 and 11–32.

Another aspect of Symeon's pastoral care was the selection and preparation of his successor. Some short time after the rebellion, Symeon sought to be relieved of his responsibilities as abbot and he began to train his disciple Arsenios to take over from him. Again, his writings show us his method: *Discourse 18* outlines the qualities he feels are necessary, based on his own formation from the Studite tradition. In this homily, he explains that ambition was not a good reason for putting yourself forward for this sort of office. Instead an abbot should be transparently devout, humble, and of blameless life; he should be a strong enough personality to be a good shepherd, but devoid of the desire for power or status, and he must hate every pleasure of the flesh and all life's comforts. He must have "the great and mystical gifts" in addition to normal Christian virtues.[21] The list of virtuous characteristics he gives reads like St. Paul's lists of the gifts of the spirit (Eph 4:7–13). They should include gentleness, absence of any lustful desires, the ability to grieve for the sins of others,

---

21. *Discourse 18*, De Catanzaro, *Discourses*, 219.

and to demonstrate "the abundant grace of the Holy Spirit enlightening the interior of your heart and making it into a very sun . . . so that you are inflamed by union with the un-approachable fire, yet not consumed thereby because your soul is set free form all passion."[22] This reference to Moses approaching the burning bush serves to assert the spiritual father's place within the "golden chain" of enlightened ones. When Symeon went into exile he was accompanied by his most loyal pupils, showing how as a spiritual father he attracted the sort of devotion he had felt towards Eulabes, both of them being spiritual fathers whose holiness had been seen through visions of light and fire. Into a new environment, where even running water was not readily available, Symeon led his "children" as if into a wilderness, in which they and he were confident he would again find God.

A good superior will avoid favorites and will enable a rich spiritual harvest through sowing good seed in his teaching. He will also administer the sacraments with reverence, a clear indication of how much Symeon valued them, giving evidence that his enthusiasm for prayer was in no way *Messalian*. The statements given in this homily, if based on his own experience, demonstrate a remarkable synthesis of good management and piety.

Spiritual Fatherhood and Authority

When evaluating the status of Symeon as spiritual father we need always to bear in mind the bias evident in Stethatos' account. There are also some unexplained aspects to the apparent commission by Symeon; why was there a thirty-year delay in starting on the biography and

22. *Discourse 18*, De Catanzaro, *Discourses*, 217.

editing the sermons? Stethatos also records a number of remarkable and miraculous events, the sort of manifestations that would be required to prove sanctity. One of the accusations levied against Symeon when he faced the Imperial synod was that he had unduly venerated Eulabes. Proofs of sanctity such as miracles would help establish the credentials of a holy man, so when Stethatos emphasizes the miraculous deeds of Symeon pre and post-mortem he is asserting Symeon's place in the golden chain—and thus his (Stethatos') own position as a link. The holiness of the prior link in the chain was crucial, and Symeon was very clear that this was demonstrated by divine illumination, hence the importance in his narrative of the visions he has in which Eulables is seen surrounded by light and in the presence of other great men of faith from the past. As he explains:

> The saints, too, are illumined in the same way [through divine light] by the divine angels . . . from generation to generation they join [their predecessors] through the practice of God's commandments. Like them, they are enlightened and received this grace of God by participation. They become just like a golden chain with each one of them a link, bound to all the preceding saints in faith, love, and good works. So it is that they become one single chain in the one God, a chain that cannot easily be broken.[23]

Establishing the credentials of your spiritual father meant that great weight was attached to his intercession for you and also the power he had to remit your sins. Both these will be explored more in chapter 5.

---

23. *Third Theological Chapters*, McGuckin, *Symeon*, 73.

The Spiritual Father as Holy Fool

Some of the aspects of Eulabes' behavior that Symeon describes resemble those of so-called "holy fools," people who deliberately adopted unconventional attitudes and activities as a means of demonstrating complete humility and rejection of the world. Being nude in public (this excludes such places as public baths and gymnasia where exercise was taken by young men in the nude) was read as a conscious rejection of social convention; indeed, it was even forbidden by canon law. Symeon goes to some lengths to point out that one of the ways in which Eulabes demonstrated his holiness was that he was unselfconscious about his naked body and the nakedness of those around him. Indeed Symeon uses this as an example of how to be a truly dispassionate man, one who has moved beyond normal human temptation. If such a man were: "to be confined with tens of thousands who were unbelieving and impious and debauched, and his naked body were to be in contact with their naked bodies, he would not be injured in his faith, nor estranged from his Master, nor forgetful of His beauty."[24] Being surrounded by nudity without being aroused by showed that you were completely dead to the world.[25] Physically he showed no more response than a corpse in the presence of another corpse, Stethatos says.[26] Eulabes as an enlightened saintly person was wholly possessed by Christ, and there was no room in him for erotic leanings towards humans. He was totally subsumed in love of the divine.[27] In the same hymn where he asserts Eulabes' innocence in these matters, he daringly refers to his own

24. *Sixth Ethical Discourse*, Golitzin, *Mystical* (vol. 2), 71.

25. *Third Theological Chapters*, McGuckin, *Symeon*, 82.

26. Greenfield, *Life*, 185.

27. *Hymn 15*, Griggs, *Divine Eros,* 89.

sexual member as being "of Christ," since his whole person belongs to Jesus and has thus been purified.[28]

Eulabes' apparent holy folly was something that caused Symeon's devotion to him to be challenged. Stephen the *Synkellos* accused him of elevating a sinner to the status of saint. As noted earlier, Basil II had taken steps to rationalize the whole process of how saints were acknowledged and venerated, by commissioning a calendar that included the canon or approved list of saints. Symeon's stubborn devotion to his father added fuel to the flames of theological controversy. The criticism by the *Synkellos* was raised by the patriarch as a reason for calling into question Symeon's judgment. Although Symeon defended himself with a catena of biblical citations and allusions, the doggedness with which he persisted in his veneration of Eulabes in circumstances that were so hostile to him could be read as an example of holy folly on his own part.

Another example of how "holy folly" is honored can be found in the story of Arsenios, the monk whom Symeon appointed as his successor. Earlier in his monastic career Arsenios had committed grave sins and on being forgiven humbled himself excessively. This appears to be one of the reasons Symeon had such faith in his suitability as his replacement as Abbot of the monastery. When Symeon instructs Arsenios he recalls the example of Eulabes.[29] As a practitioner of holy folly and an advocate of it Symeon willingly accepted the humiliation that was the church's response to him. Far more important to him than any worldly status or recognition was that he was able to experience God directly, in mystical encounters which were what affirmed the authority of Eulabes. This is our next topic.

28. *Hymn 15*, Griggs, *Divine Eros,* 87–88.
29. Greenfield, *Life*, 135–45.

FOUR

Mysticism and Divine Light

What is Mysticism?

As noted in chapter 1, Symeon is often associated with the concept of mysticism, and some see him as paving the way for a big movement in medieval Eastern Christianity, the *hesychast* revival, which peaked in the fourteenth century just before the collapse of the Byzantine empire to the Turkish Muslim forces. Symeon's influence on *hesychasm* will be considered in more detail in the concluding chapter. For now, we need to consider what mysticism is and why George Maloney, one of the earliest modern commentators on Symeon, chose to describe him as a "mystic of fire and light." First, what is meant by mysticism? A colloquial understanding of the word suggests things that are strange or unexplained. Looking at the root of the word itself throws more light on the subject. The Greek *mystikos* comes from a verb (*myein*) that means to close the mouth or eyes. By sealing off two of the most obvious physical channels thorough which humans engage with the world around them the hidden, inner life comes to the fore, and for religious people this can lead to a deeper engagement with God than can be attained through simply verbal or intellectual processes. For the Christian, mysticism might be summed up by the desire: "That they all may be one, even as You, Father, are in me, and I am in You" (John 17:21). St. Paul writes that: "The one who adheres to God becomes one spirit" (1 Cor 6:17), one spirit with God and one spirit with other believers, both living and among the faithful departed. Within diverse religious traditions, mysticism connotes a sharing in God's spirit. Mysticism suggests an understanding of matters that cannot be explained, except perhaps through means that transcend the conventional limitations of human perception. Because mysticism is highly experiential it tends to be individualist and may therefore sit outside the parameters of organized structures such as the established church. In the case of Symeon, his insistence that Eulabes' holiness was demonstrated by association with visions of divine light, and Symeon's own many experiences of ecstatic "mystical" *theophanies*, led him into conflict with the established church. Symeon ultimately believed that true spiritual authority, even amounting to the power to remit sin, resided in those who had undergone mystical encounters with God—even if they had not received the official blessing of the established church through the sacrament of ordination. The defining political battle of his life grew from his conviction that mystical encounters proved authentic spiritual life (and thus conferred authority) in the face of those representing the imperial court and the church who felt that he lacked discernment in the matter of his devotion to his spiritual father. His accusers believed that

A Guide to St. Symeon the New Theologian

by insisting Eulabes was spiritually enlightened through mystical encounters Symeon eroded the authority of the state, by criticizing those he felt were attempting to teach and preach without the benefit of spiritual enlightenment. That he made such criticisms is uncontested. His *Ethical Discourses* and *Hymns* in particular resound with comments like this:

> Tell me, how do you not tremble to speak about God?
> How dare you, you who are yourself all flesh,
> And have not yet become spirit like Paul,
> To speak or to philosophize about the Spirit?[1]

His moral outrage about what he saw as spiritual ignorance, arrogance, even, was unconstrained and led to his removal from his own position of authority. To some extent the situation was complicated by socio-political matters, such as the relative status of monasteries and non-monastic secular churches, and the complex interplay of class, money, and patronage within both Symeon's monasteries and the Byzantine court. Whatever you decide about this, though, it is important to understand on what basis Symeon was invoking the authority of mysticism. For most of his life he was a monk and as already noted the monastic life focused round prayer and contemplation based on knowledge of the Bible, predominantly the Psalms, and also the Gospels and Pauline letters. This is where we need to start.

Biblical Sources for Mysticism

Both Judaism and Christianity are based on narratives about humanity discovering the will of God, and working

1. *Hymn 21*, Griggs, *Divine Eros,* 147.

out how to fulfil this in their daily lives. Yet neither of these faiths suggests that it is possible for mere men and women to experience the godhead directly. The power of God was therefore mediated through holy beings such as angels and prophets and through individuals experiencing visions, dreams or other unusual states of consciousness in which they receive special insight. In the Old Testament prophets such as Moses have a key role as intermediaries between the two, acting as the "mouth" of God; they were permitted to be in the presence of God even while he remained invisible. In Christianity the gap between man and God is bridged by the Incarnation, the sending by God the Father of his Son in the form of a man, Jesus Christ (John 1:14). In both the Old and New Testaments angels are used to carry messages from God to humanity (the Greek word *angellos* from which we get the word "angel," meaning messenger). In both Testaments fire and light are used to signify the presence of God. In Judaism God cannot be represented by any image, as this offends the prohibition against idols. And when men such as the prophet Moses do approach God they cannot see him. (Exodus 33:20 states: "But He said, 'You cannot see My face; for no man can see My face and live.'") Exodus, however, records God revealing himself through a pillar of cloud and fire: "Moreover, God led them, by day in a pillar of cloud to show them the way, and by night in a pillar of fire. Thus the pillar of cloud by day and the pillar of fire by night did not depart from them before all the people" (Exod 13:21–22). This enabled the exodus, or flight, of the chosen people of God from Egypt, led by Moses. In Exodus 3:1–6, Moses was tending a flock of sheep and approached the mountain of Horeb, "the mountain of God." Here the Angel of the Lord appeared to him "in a flame of fire in the midst of a bush"; the fire did not consume the bush, however. Moses heard God calling to him from inside the fire, telling him that he stood on holy ground: "Moses hid his face, for he was afraid to look at God." Lastly, "when Moses came down from Mount Sinai (and the two tablets were in Moses' hands when he came down from the mountain), he did not know the skin of his face was glorified while God talked with Him" (Exod 34:29). So, God is shown by fire; being in his presence creates refulgence or glowing of the face of the man who approaches him. This is mirrored in the New Testament, above all in one key passage describing an occasion when Jesus' face and clothes became effulgent.

A key role of New Testament theology is to establish the identity of Jesus Christ and understand his relationship to the Father and the Holy Spirit as co-eternal members of the Holy Trinity. As Jesus himself was Jewish many of his statements about his identity, and the parts of the narrative of his life that focus on his Sonship, frequently mention Old Testament figures, especially Moses and Elijah. The transfiguration of Christ is a case in point (Matt 17:1–9; Mark 9:2–10; Luke 9:28–31). This text describes a *theophany* through Christ's divine, uncreated energy. The Synoptic Gospels describe how Jesus took Peter, James, and John to the top of the mountain where he was transfigured before their eyes, his face shining like the sun and his robes glowing as white as light. Also on top of the mountain appeared the figures of Moses and Elijah. The presence of these two great figures from the Old Testament signifies to Orthodox Christians the "great cloud of witnesses" referred to in Hebrews 12:1. They also tie in with references throughout the New Testament to Jesus' Messiahship as being foretold in the Hebrew Scriptures and fulfilled in the new covenant. In the Eastern Christian tradition the transfiguration, celebrated on August 8th, is a major feast day, indicating how important it is for Orthodox Christians to acknowledge the role of the Spirit in making manifest God to humankind.

Christian Appropriation of the Term "Mystery"

The word "mystery" was used in pre-Christian religions, such as the mystery cults, but early Christian writers, especially those with a philosophical training, such as Clement of Alexandria in the second century, began to apply the concept specifically to Christian experience of God.[2] Although originally applied to interpretation of the Bible, it soon became used to denote a direct encounter with God, a union that did not require the structures of the church or any rule book. As such it lent itself readily to the monastic life where silent contemplation, based on knowledge by heart of the Scriptures, formed the bulk of men's spiritual life day by day, leading to the "vision" of God through dreams, visions, and other ecstatic experiences. However, ancient Christians would not have seen themselves as mystics or necessarily used the term themselves. Post-Enlightenment, there was a desire to find names for and categorize religious and other forms of experience. Prior to that, medieval scholastics aimed to apply a forensic style of analysis to the religious life. Scholars such as Stephen the Synkellos were keen to apply logic and rational approaches to theological matters. Symeon, by contrast, believed that authentic authority came from the inner experience of God, the direct "mystical" encounter he describes in his visions of light and which he found in the witness of his spiritual father Eulabes. Because he valued the holy sacraments, he did not believe that just because a man had been ordained and therefore legitimately empowered to

2. McGinn, "Mysticism," 19–25.

administer the sacraments such a man was automatically holy. Indeed, he writes disparagingly about the corruption of clergy, and how they effectively relinquished spiritual authority by succumbing to worldly temptations, resulting in authentic power being limited to holy men among the monastic orders. His *Letter on Confession* explains how spiritual power came to be transferred from ordained to non-ordained men. Originally "only the bishops had that authority to bind and loose [sins] which they had received in succession to the Apostles." However, the bishops became "useless," he argues, hence the authority was passed on to "priests of blameless life and worthy of divine grace. Then also, when the latter had become polluted, . . . it was transferred . . . to God's elect people, I mean to the monks."[3] The higher orders had been contaminated by "spirits of deceit and by vain and empty titles."

So what informed Symeon's understanding of mysticism, apart from his own ecstatic *theophanies*? As we have shown, the Bible was the starting point, and patristic exegesis of this also nourished the monastic tradition. Some of the greatest early church fathers were educated in Hellenistic philosophy and culture, so they wove together Christian and Neoplatonic ideas. Gregory of Nyssa's *Life of Moses*, written in the second half of the fourth century, combines insights from the narrative of Moses on Mount Sinai recorded in Exodus 33:20 with a famous passage in Part Seven of Book 7 of Plato's *Republic*, in which the philosopher envisages a cave in which prisoners are held. Plato suggests that for years they can see the flickering shadows of figures cast onto the wall by the light of a fire within the cave. They may assume these are "real" figures and when they finally come out into the light of day for the first time they see the actual forms of physical things

3. *Letter on Confession*, Golitzin, *Mystical* (vol. 3), 196.

as they are. The shadows represent an immature and deluded understanding of the world. Any who exit the cave are so overwhelmed by the brightness they can't see any of the things they are now told are "real"; by contrast, the things they had believed to be so are no more than shadows and illusions. Nyssa's account of the life of the great prophet is a Christian interpretation of the process of finding God through a spiritual ascent, mimicking Moses' repeated ascents up the holy mountain, Sinai (also known in the Torah as Horeb), which features prominently in Exodus. Sinai became a hugely significant holy place for Christian monasticism, especially it was the location of St. Catherine's monastery, which was the home of one of the most influential of Eastern Christian writers, the seventh-century Abbot John Climacus.

Gregory's text may have been read by the anonymous *Pseudo-Dionysius*, who suggests in his *Mystical Theology* that true union with God is through an "ascent" beyond the medium of language to wordless adoration of God. The original Dionysius the Areopagite is referred to in Acts 17:34. According to this text, St. Paul was preaching in Athens and as well as being challenged by the Jews in the synagogue he was verbally attacked by Stoic and Epicurean philosophers. His preaching made a number of converts and one of them, named Dionysius the Areopagite, decided to break from philosophy to follow Paul's Christian message. The fifth/sixth-century Syrian who wrote under the name of this Dionysius includes in his writings a good deal of Neoplatonic thought combined with exaltation of the main rituals and sacraments of the Christian church. Much of his writing suggests there are inherently cosmic hierarchies, such as those of the angels (angels, archangels, seraphim, and cherubim) or the threefold orders of the church through the ordained roles of deacon, priest, and bishop. For the Christian to engage with the top of the hierarchy they must "ascend," metaphorically. This image is commonly found in Christian literature; the John Climacus mentioned above was so-called because a Greek word for a leaning ladder or staircase is *klimax*, and his key text was known as *The Ladder of Divine Ascent*.

Pseudo-Dionysius' *The Mystical Theology* is perhaps one of the most exciting and baffling six pages of writing in the Christian canon. It starts with a petition to the Trinity to lead the reader "up to the farthest, highest peak of mystic Scripture" and ends by asserting that the "supreme Cause of every perceptual thing" cannot itself be conceived of. In other words, God cannot be understood by any of the physical means of perception which he created; climbing higher (as he puts it) means that you only come to understand God by being able to say what he is not. The brief text ends:

> There is no speaking of it [the supreme Cause], nor name nor knowledge of it. Darkness and light, error and truth—it is none of these. It is beyond assertion and denial. We make assertions and denials of what is next to it, but never of it, for it is both beyond every assertion, being the perfect and unique cause of all things, and, by virtue of its pre-eminently simple and absolute nature, free of every limitation, beyond every limitation; it is also beyond denial.[4]

This concept of meaning being only comprehensible through *apophasis* (absence or transcending of speech) gave its name to a whole thread of theology, the *apophatic* tradition or *Via Negativa* as it is usually known in Western Christianity, where it is associated with *St. John of the Cross*. In his text Dionysius starts by explaining that

4. Luibheid, *Pseudo-Dionysius*, 135–41.

Scripture has hidden meanings that can be mystically explained by the church. Like Gregory of Nyssa he uses the figure of Moses climbing Mount Sinai to encounter God as a symbolic representation of how the human soul "ascends" towards God through stages of purification, leading to ever deepening enlightenment. Paradoxically, although Jesus is God's "Word" and it is through words that Scripture is recorded and through language that we make sense of both the physical and spiritual world, mysticism implies that conventional language must been left behind; that it is too limited to express the extraordinary experience of being incorporated in God.

Pseudo-Dionysius's ideas were likely drawn on by the author (also anonymous!) of the great Western medieval text *The Cloud of Unknowing*, written in the 1380s, which talks about the encounter with God being in the "cloud," the darkness of non-knowing. St. John of the Cross's "dark night of the soul" picks up on this image of enlightenment through absence of light, another paradox in which it is through cloud or darkness that true insight is gained.

Implicit in the language of union with God, of *deification*, is the human hunger for such intimacy. The longed-for union with God is described in erotic language that may be startling, because to the modern mind the word "eros" suggests physical, carnal love. English has a number of ways to express passion and affection; we have charity, desire, loving kindness, and affection, as well as "love." In Greek there are several different words that can be translated as love, including *agape, philia* (from which we get the word philanthropy, meaning love for humanity), and *eros*. Latin brings *amor, caritas,* and *dilectio* in to the mix! Origen's *Commentary on Song of Songs* explained how language could be used allegorically to convey layers of meaning which were accessible in different ways to people at different stages of spiritual development. *Eros* denotes appetitive love, a yearning for union that, if one puts aside the human sexual version of such union, well describes the hunger a spiritual person has for God. And while God is not conceived of as having needs and appetites, which would make him dependent on humans, the image of sexual faithfulness is also used in the Judaeo-Christian tradition to show that God is jealous for men's whole attention; they must not commit the idolatry of following strange gods and being unfaithful to the covenantal relationship established between God and humanity through Moses, Abraham, and other Old Testament patriarchs and prophets. But we are not used to love of God being expressed in erotic words, and this is perhaps why some of the expressions used by Symeon can seem very dramatic to our ears.

Hesychasm and Mysticism

As we will see in the concluding chapter of this study, Symeon's mysticism had far-reaching consequences, being a key feature in the late medieval renewal of interest in this mystical way of understanding God. Although fourteenth-century hesychasm as it became known contains very specific philosophical and abstract formulae (to do with the "essence" and "energies" of God) that are not dominant in Symeon's writings, his sense that God had to be experienced in ways beyond the purely rational, that this could be through visions of uncreated light, provided rich pickings for the development of a mystical tradition. (As an aside, there are some references in Symeon's writings to the division between essence and energies of God. For example, in *Hymn 28* and *Hymn 23* he distinguishes between the intelligible and unintelligible light, also expressed as sensible and insensible).

Hesychia means rest, stillness; by association silence, solitude, and tranquillity. It is the antithesis of being overly engaged in public life and denotes a withdrawing into the self, a letting go of the things of the world in order to find communion with God. Hesychasm was practised by desert hermits, though they might not have called themselves hesychasts; this more technical term is more associated with the teachings of Gregory Palamas, discussed in chapter 6. St. Antony, the very first known monk, withdrew into the desert to escape the encroachment of the world on his spiritual life. Apparently he experienced a down-pouring of light as he heard the voice of Christ calling him into service. Athanasius' biography of him records this: in the solitude of his cell the hermit was wrestling with demons that had taken the form of wild beasts; Antony rebukes them and at that moment it was as if the roof of his cell were opened and he saw a ray of light dropping down, to the horror of the demons who vanish immediately.[5] This recalls the story in Mark 2:4 where Jesus' disciples remove the roof of a room in which a sick man is waiting for healing. Antony's experience of seeking and finding God through solitude was a massive influence on the development of monasticism, so his experience of light is especially valued. Symeon's insistence that monks commune with God through direct, personal encounters in addition to partaking of the sacraments could be seen as a form of *hesychasm*. His renunciation of the world (common for all monks) and criticism of the court (rather more of a special feature of Symeon's writings) also suggest the practise of *hesychasm* was one to which he was sympathetic.

5. Athanasius, *Life*, 10.1

Symeon as a Mystic

Symeon's place within this tradition of mysticism is significant. Like all monks, whether in the East or West, his primary engagement with God came through saturation in the Scriptures and he was not a hermit: daily celebration of the Eucharist in the company of his fellow monks was a crucial part of his worship and spiritual life. Indeed his homilies, which have come down to us as "catecheses" or teachings of the faith, were preached within the context of communal monasticism, and even in his exile he was accompanied by some other monks. The sacraments, as already mentioned, were very important to him. It is through consuming the body and blood of Christ that a Christian becomes literally incorporated in God. Baptism, for Symeon, signified the first initiation into and demonstration of belonging to the Christian family; metaphorically a second baptism of tears was the way to maintain the purity necessary for the vision of God. However, on this bedrock of Scripture and sacrament Symeon built his Christian life using visions of divine light. We have already learned from the outline of his life how visions of light and images of fire permeate his writings. Even his initiation into monastic life is colored by the visions of light experienced by "George"; indeed one could almost say that his identity was shaped by mystical encounters. It was visions of light that first opened his spiritual eyes (very much like St. Paul, temporarily blinded as he received inner light on the Damascus Road) and which cemented his attachment to his spiritual father once he was in the monastery. In *Discourse* 35 he describes two visions of light, first to the elder and then to his novice: first he describes how Eulabes shone "with The divine glory" when he approached him and clasped his feet.[6] Then, in the first person, Symeon shows how this *theophany* then spread to the novice at his feet. In turn, the person of the elder fades away as the focus moves to the young Symeon's own experience. He describes a number of physical sensations associated with light and fire: "At once I perceived a divine warmth. Then a small radiance that shone forth. Then a divine breath from his words. Then a fire kindled in my heart, which caused constant streams of tears to flow. After that a fine beam went through my mind more quickly than lightning."[7]

It is only at that point that the narrative returns to consider the role of Eulabes again: "Then there appeared to me as it were a light in the night and a small flaming cloud resting on his head, while I lay on my face and made supplication. Afterwards it moved away and shortly afterwards appeared to me as being in heaven."[8]

So what we have here is first of all awareness that Eulabes was already "illuminated" and then a description of how that illumination literally spread through the person of his devoted pupil. The occasion is a compelling combination of "out of body" vision and the highly tangible sensations of warmth and air. The "living saint" illuminated the pupil just as one fragment of burning kindling lights another piece.

As he developed as an abbot Symeon strengthened his conviction that experiencing God directly through visions demonstrated inner illumination: "There is no other way for anyone to know about God unless it is by means of the contemplation of the light which is sent by Him," he

6. De Catanzaro, *Discourses*, 363.

7. De Catanzaro, *Discourses*, 363 and *Discourse 17*, De Catanzaro, *Discourses*, 205.

8. *Discourse 35*, De Catanzaro, *Discourses*, 363.

declared.[9] His teachings to his monks explain what this might feel like, and how to achieve it. In the *First Ethical Discourse* he compares the acquisition of spiritual insight to a man who after "sitting for so many years in his light-less prison" is gradually able to see the blue sky as a hole is made in the roof of his cell and slowly enlarged. (This seems to echo the image of Plato's cave.) In just the same way, he says, someone who finally achieves "the vision of the spiritual life" after many years of darkness realizes how limited their old life was, and in time begins to live "in the light." He extends the allegory to suggest the whole world is a dark prison, outside of which is "the light of the Sun in Three Persons, the light which transcends word and thought and every created light."[10] But he does not merely extol this as a desirable spiritual encounter. Spiritual illu-mination is, he argues, essential to spiritual authority. He continues his argument in the same homily by asking a series of rhetorical questions: "You who ignore everything we have been saying, and who have not arrived yourselves at the perception and knowledge and experience of divine illumination and contemplation, how can you talk or write at all about such things without shuddering?"[11] It is akin to someone pretending to act as a judge without any formal training or legitimate appointment; in other words, with-out the spiritual experience that comes from training and mystical *theophany* you have no power and more impor-tantly no authority to heal and counsel others.

Another example of his teaching on light can be found in the *Tenth Ethical Discourse*. Here he attacks those who claim that Jesus is the Light of the World (John 8:12) but do not have that light within them by being conscious

9. *Fifth Ethical Discourse*, Golitzin, *Mystical* (vol. 2), 52.

10. Golitzin, *Mystical* (vol. 1), 75–77.

11. Ibid., 79.

of the indwelling of Christ in them. His tone is vehement, shocking: those who are unaware of having been touched by God are barely alive:

> If He is light, therefore, but we say that those who are clothed with Him do not perceive Him, in what respect do we differ from a corpse? If He is the vine and we are the branches, unless we clearly know our union with Him, we are soulless wood, fruitless and withered, matter which is fit for the unquenchable fire.[12]

Ignorance of enlightenment is akin to nudity, he warns; it is only appropriate for outcasts from society. He uses the image of being "clothed in Christ" (Gal 3:27) to remind his readers that having made a commitment to Jesus Christ they have become incorporated into union with God, and not being aware of this is truly shameful: "He then who has put on God, will he not recognize with his intellect and see what he has clothed himself with? . . . Only the dead feel nothing when they are clothed, and I am very much afraid that those who say such things are the ones who are really and truly dead and naked."[13]

The experience of *deification*, being "clothed" in Christ, is like wearing the right sort of wedding garment (Matt 22:1); it is a mark of spiritual maturity. Not being conscious of this extraordinary blessing is an insult to God's gracious mercy: "All who have not been clothed with Christ (Gal 3:27), that is, those who have not received the light . . . will appear naked and will be filled with much shame from every quarter."[14] The references to nudity are especially pertinent as one of the accusations levied against

12. *Tenth Ethical Discourse*, Goltizin, *Mystical* (vol. 1), 161, 165–66.

13. *Fifth Ethical Discourse*, Golitzin, *Mystical* (vol. 2), 46.

14. Discourse 28, De Catanzaro, *Discourses*, 299.

Eulabes and thus Symeon's respect for him was that he behaved as a *salos* or holy fool, as discussed earlier.

The burning bush in the Moses narrative involves not only light but fire, and this is another metaphor used by Symeon to suggest the presence of God. Exodus 13:21–22 provides the image of God leading his chosen people in the form of a pillar of cloud by day and of fire by night. Luke 12:49 prefigures the fire that descends as the Holy Spirit at Pentecost. In one of his *Hymns* Symeon constructs a dialogue; he asks his spiritual father how he might safely travel towards God.

> "Light a big fire," he said, "and I will walk into the middle,
> And if I do not remain unburned, may you not follow me!" . . .
> . . . He brought me nearer, he took me in his arms,
> And again he kissed me with a holy kiss,
> And the whole of him spread the scent of immortality."[15]

This conversation also alludes to the three holy Chaldeans (Shadrach, Meshach, and Abednego) who were placed in the furnace as punishment for refusing to worship idols and who were not consumed by the flames (Dan 3:13–24). By this image Symeon exhorts his monks to leave the old way of the material world behind and to show commitment to their new calling. Akin to the idea of light spreading light from one disciple to another is the image of flames catching kindling, an effective way of describing souls that were primed and just needed a spark to bring them alive. His *Seventh Ethical Discourse* elaborates on this, describing how God is like a fire that takes hold and "in those in whom it is kindled, it rises

15. *Hymn 18*, Griggs, *Divine Eros,* 124.

up into a great flame and reaches to the heaven."[16] As in the biblical models, the fire does not consume or destroy what it burns; rather it purifies it. Only the "evil thoughts like thorns" are consumed and the light created by the fire enables the ascetic to see into his soul and recognize God within him. Light and fire are connected in another way in Symeon's writings. Much of the light he describes is that which comes from fire, as in the account of the burning bush already discussed. *Hymn 22* describes God showing himself as "a flame, and He is seen as a ray and a fire."[17]

In some places Symeon combines fire and light as separate images, for example in *Hymn 25*, lines 33–35:

> But what exaltation of light! Oh but the movements of fire,
> Oh but the swirling flame in me, the wretch,
> Light that operates by You and by your glory.[18]

The elemental physicality of both fire and light is important; it both reminds the reader that they should be seeking total transformation, of their souls and bodies, and that a transcendent God uses many different, non-verbal means, to communicate to his faithful.

Symeon as Theologian

By now it should be clear that Symeon believed you should only speak from experience, and that consciousness of the divine indwelling alone gave validity to your authority. But he did not restrict his concern to explaining how personal *theophanies* could be interpreted as part of individual

16. *Seventh Ethical Discourse*, Golitzin, *Mystical* (vol. 2), 98–99.
17. Griggs, *Divine Eros,* 163.
18. Ibid., 194.

salvation. He was also concerned to explain theological doctrine; being a poet he used light imagery here, too. His *Third Theological Chapter* contains one of his most dramatic sequences of light imagery and it is all focused on an extensive doctrinal argument for the unity of the Trinity. The text contains conventional Gospel proof-texts and a typically personal invocation to the Holy Spirit as the "remedy of sin and gateway of all repentance." He briefly depicts the Trinity as the divergent waters of a river coming from a single stream, and then for a couple of pages the text collapses into an ecstatic eulogy of God as light, in which the images come so thick and fast it is almost impossible to analyze them accurately. First, he describes as light each of the persons of the Trinity, the Father, the Son, and the Holy Spirit. Then he refers to the shared nature of the divine essence, suggesting they are "one single light as they are simple, non-composite, timeless, eternal, and possessed of the same honor and glory." Next he raises the Father as the source of all light, with everything "given to us as arising from the light." Finally, he lists a series of concrete and abstract nouns—life, immortality, the bridal chamber, the garments of the saints, his resurrection. These are all compared to light, after which he gives a whole string of scriptural references describing "the comforter, the pearl, the seed of mustard, the true vine" as light. After a further discussion of the "energies" of God (a notion we shall explore in chapter 6) he continues in more poetic mode: "His goodness is light; his compassion . . . his mercy, his embrace, his watchful care are light. His scepter is light, his crook, and his consolation."[19]

Discourse 36 contains a more discrete focus on the incarnation. Having praised God for the experience of being guided by a spiritually illumined man, he explains

19. *Third Theological Discourse*, McGuckin, *Symeon*, 138–39.

that as a result he now experiences visions of light himself. He is able to see God flashing around his "feeble eyes with the undefiled splendor of Thy countenance"; the invisible is rendered visible. While he continued to experience the "lightnings that were flashing about me" he felt himself being "washed with luminous water."[20] This incarnational motif is repeated later in the same homily. His conviction of the authority conferred by experiencing light visions is repeated in front of an icon of the Virgin. He describes how, after a period of joyful weeping resulting from a visionary experience, he goes to venerate the "spotless ikon of her who bore Thee." While he was on the ground in front of the icon he feels his heart has been transformed into light, "and then I knew that I have Thee consciously within me." The deeper love he now feels for God is not due to a memorial of his sacrifice but because "I in very truth believed that I had Thee, substantial love, within me." Through the physicality of tears, light, the contact of his body on the ground, his inner being and heart are saturated by knowing God's love as "substantial."[21] This is no mere intellectual abstraction, it is not the empty theologizing of theorists who have not encountered God in this visceral way.

A final case study is Symeon's use of light in *Discourse 23*. The homily starts with conventional exhortations to turn aside from sin and discover the joy that is given through spiritual healing. The final few sections are ostensibly on mystical intoxication and present repentance as a spiritual winepress. One image here is developed in a most complex and subtle manner. The passage reads:

20. *Discourse* 36, De Catanzaro, *Discourses*, 372 and 373.
21. *Discourse* 36, De Catanzaro, *Discourses*, 376.

> As the Spirit presses and filters his heart [as in a winepress], so it produces a joy that is genuine and unmixed with affliction. For this reason death will have no dominion over it—no blemish will be found in it. But it will be like wine that has been strained and is held up against the sun[light] shining brilliantly and showing its color more clearly and flashing joyfully on the face of him who drinks it as he faces the sun.[22]

To explain this Symeon describes the sensations and intellectual processes he experiences when contemplating this type of light. The theological interpretation will come later. The color and the luminosity of the wine are stressed, and he ponders which of the aesthetic and sensuous qualities please him most:

> I do not know which pleases me the more, the sight of the sun's rays and the delight of their purity, or the drinking and the taste of the wine in my mouth. I would say it is the latter, yet the former attracts me and appears more pleasant to me. Yet as I look at it, I derive more pleasure from the sweetness of tasting, so that I am not sated with seeing nor filled from drinking. For when I think that I have drunk my fill, then the beauty of the rays that pass through it redoubles my thirst and I crave it again. The more I am eager to fill my stomach, my mouth burns ten times as much and I am inflamed by the thirst and desire for that most transparent drink.[23]

This must surely be a reference to the living water of John 4:14 and John 6:36. But he does not just talk about the thirst-quenching qualities of wine: the glowing wine

22. *Discourse* 23, De Catanzaro, *Discourses*, 257–58.

23. *Discourse* 23, De Catanzaro, *Discourses*, 258.

remains a luminous entity, because humans have bodies as well as souls and this is why light (like water, wine, heat, scent, touch, and so on) is a means by which they can understanding God's presence. Furthermore, the light is also otherworldly, it is *apophatic*; he connects the physical, almost domestic, image of sunlight passing through wine to the more abstract and spiritual versions of light he talks of elsewhere as epiphanies of God. From gazing into a cup held up to the sun (in itself perhaps a memory of Eucharistic celebration?) he shifts into an analysis that combines the transfiguration, a *Desert Fathers'* legend about a holy hermit's fingers becoming fiery torches, and the beginnings of a Trinitarian motif: the light passing through the wine is one ray that does not separate off from the light source. There is a unity between the different aspects of the light, as there is unity in the three persons of the Holy Trinity. It is an extraordinarily rich and complex use of sources, genre, ideas, and language:

> the shining of the wine and the beam of the sun
> as they shine on the face of him who drinks
> penetrate to his inward parts, to his hands, his
> feet, his back, and transform him wholly into
> fire. They give him the power to burn and melt
> the enemies that approach him from every side.
> He becomes dear to the sunlight and a friend
> of the sun. To the transparent wine belonging
> to the rays that issue from it he becomes like a
> beloved son, for the drink is his nourishment
> purging the infection of his putrified flesh.[24]

Symeon seems unable to separate the fire and the sunlight from his physical being, an indivisibility of elements which mirrors the inextricably meshed humanity and divinity in Christ, or the *perichoresis* of the Trinity.

24. *Discourse 23*, De Catanzaro, *Discourses*, 258.

A Guide to St. Symeon the New Theologian

What he describes (with false humility) as his inability to "understand" whether the sun or the wine is better is, in fact, an *apophatic* reading of the vision of God: it goes beyond words and reason into sensation and instinct. This complete integration of the divine empowers the one who experiences it. Directly experiencing God's love and forgiveness through the immediacy of the non-verbal, un-created light grants the charism and authority to transmit forgiveness to others. As we know Symeon insisted that if are not enlightened you are "unable either to lead others or to teach them the will of God," and this means, specifically, that you are not "fit to hear (in confession) the thoughts of others."[25] In *Discourse 23* he asserts his authority as abbot by going back to the image of fear of God and repentance as the mystical winepress, in a direct address to his "beloved children." This is an extraordinarily sophisticated and theological use of what seems like a familiar image. Stephen of Alexina's criticism of him as incapable of theological argument seems misplaced indeed.

Reception of Symeon's Mysticism

Symeon's mysticism was not universally applauded; indeed mysticism in general was viewed with considerable suspicion by the established church, and some have suggested that Symeon's teachings verged on the *heterodox* if not actually schismatic. Some religious groups designated as heretics placed great emphasis on the inner vision and the imperative that holiness of life superseded structured forms of authority. *Messalians* (who were condemned by the Council of Ephesus in 431) held that the devil could only be driven out of the world by incessant prayer;

25. *Discourse 33*, De Catanzaro, *Discourses*, 340.

nothing else—neither sacraments, the established church, ordination—was efficacious. They led a nomadic and *mendicant* lifestyle. Clearly this was not true of Symeon, whose teaching is very much aimed at monks in settled communities where the Eucharist was celebrated regularly. Closer in time to Symeon were the *Bogomils*. Their offence in the eyes of the establishment was more that they espoused what reads like an early experiment in socialism, which subverted the authority of not only clergy but imperial officials. About the time Symeon was born, a priest named Cosmas reported of the Bogomils that: "they teach their adherents not to submit to authority: they slander the rich: they hate the emperors: they mock their superiors and insult their lords: they claim that God has horror of those who work for emperors and recommend that all servants not work for their masters."[26]

This, also, is not an appropriate accusation to place at Symeon's door. While he does criticise the court and even shows disrespect to its officials he does so because of their corruption, because they have been seduced by worldly values and have turned their backs on God's way. And far from rejecting those in high social classes, he cooperated with them, receiving patronage from wealthy landowners in his attempts to re-build his monasteries, in addition to holding on to his own private wealth, which he put at the disposal of his monastic houses.

The final heresy of which Symeon was sometimes accused was *Pelagianism*. Pelagius was famed for a debate with Augustine about the nature of grace. Pelagius claimed that as humanity was created good it had the capacity to choose the right way to achieve salvation and did not necessarily need divine grace to assist in this. Again, this does not match Symeon's experience and teaching. He describes

26. Cosmas the Priest, *Traité*, 86.

himself as utterly dependent on the example and prayers of his holy father for guidance on his path towards salvation; to claim to be strong enough to find the right route without much spiritual support would be inconceivable to Symeon. He did, however, insist each individual must make strenuous efforts to find spiritual enlightenment. But they could only achieve *deification* through God's mercy and the intercessory prayers of the spiritual father.

As we have seen, Symeon's light and fire mysticism does not detract from or refute doctrinal teaching. Quite the reverse; in places he uses this long tradition of visionary encounter to affirm the church's teachings about the Trinity and the incarnation. His poetic rhapsodies are woven into his writings together with theological interpretation, moral exhortation, and pastoral guidance. He writes to his monks who are gathered under his care, and while he chastises those who attempt to theologize in ignorance of personal experience of God's indwelling, he does not set himself up as an authority for any other reason than that he was blessed with having been taught by a spiritual father who had himself found God in this way. He claims no special merit under his own strength, but rather repeats his reliance on the prayers and intercessions of the holy man who dragged him from the mire and set him on the path to salvation. Once established in the ascetic life, every monk needs to strengthen his commitment by constant penitence, and the sharing of his evil thoughts and deeds so that he may be renewed each day for God's service.

Penitent Tears and Confession

Two of the hallmarks of Symeon's teaching were that the constant repentance for sin that was standard monastic practice should be expressed through weeping, and that sinful urges should be disclosed to a truly holy man whose purity of life on its own was sufficient to release you from sin. Of the possible modes of confession practiced in monasteries, the most contentious was the constant (daily if not hourly) disclosure of thoughts, feelings, and intentions to the spiritual father. In requiring this of his monks Symeon was in line with the Studite tradition. However, his emphasis on the *conscious* nature of penitent tears and his use of them as a benchmark for spiritual illumination regardless of whether the spiritual father in question was ordained or not caused much unease in the church of his day. As we have seen, the term "spiritual father" could be applied both to the overall "father" of the monastery (i.e., the abbot) and to the individual mentor or guide appointed by him for the more closely worked "formation" of novices. This chapter will look at Symeon's teachings on tears and confession and explain why he felt they were so authoritative. As always, because Symeon worked very much within an established tradition, our starting place is some centuries earlier.

The Bible and Desert Fathers on Weeping

The very earliest monks, the "fathers" who withdrew to the deserts, were very familiar with the practice of weeping for penitence and awareness of sin. They had in mind examples of penitential weeping in the Gospels; for example, Peter, who "wept bitterly" when the cock crew three times, reminding him of Jesus' prophecy that he would deny him three times (Matt 26:75). John's Gospel explicitly rehabilitates Peter from his three-fold denial of Christ by balancing it with a three-fold affirmation of faith. In his post-resurrection appearance to his disciples Jesus asked Peter three times if he loved him and only on receiving his penitent assurance each time did he entrust him with "feeding his sheep" (John 21:17).

Another key paradigm for the power of penitent tears is found in the account of the so-called "sinful woman" of Luke 7:35–45, who bathed Jesus' feet with her tears and wiped them with her hair. Jesus uses her lowly actions as a paradigm for repentance and forgiveness. The righteous Pharisaic Simon at whose house she appeared uninvited was shocked by her behavior. She was a loose woman; surely Jesus should realize how inappropriate it was for her to be there and behave in such a way, he suggested. On the contrary, Jesus replied she had more need of forgiveness than his socially acceptable but proud host and had shown greater love by her actions than he had. Her grief about her former way of life could only be expressed through tears and by washing Jesus' feet with them; she humbled herself utterly. In hot dry climates feet were readily soiled by dust, animal droppings, and other foul debris, so the hospitable thing to do was to wash guests' feet on arrival at your home, preferably in flowing water so that the dirty dregs could be poured away elsewhere, referred to in Psalm 60:8. To use your own tears and your hair to clean someone's feet was an extraordinary and controversial act. In both these examples it was the penitence of the one who cried which effected their salvation.

For monks, grieving for sin was not just an expression of some individualistic sense of regretting personal misdeeds; it was penitence on behalf of all humanity. The archetypal *Desert Father*, St. Antony, writes to his brother monks about the great "grief" he feels on their behalf. Symeon uses similar terminology. The healing effected by penitence expressed in this way was acknowledged in the tradition; one of the anonymous sayings of the *Desert Fathers* simply reports: "An old man said, 'Let us weep, brethren, and let our eyes stream with tears, before we go there where our tears shall burn up our bodies.'"[1]

Evagrius

As well as being shaped by the *Desert Fathers* Symeon's insistence on the need for tearful repentance owes much to Evagrius, whose writings for monks exerted a great influence on the later ascetic tradition. Evagrius was a fourth-century monk who was much inspired by Greek philosophy and the works of Origen, an influence that may have contributed to some aspects of his teaching (predominantly Christological ones) being condemned by the Fifth Ecumenical Church Council in 553. The teachings of both

1. #126, Wortley, *Anonymous*, 81.

men were misinterpreted, even misunderstood, and their works were suppressed, more by the Latin church than the Greek one. In the case of Evagrius, his writings only survived by being attributed to other writers not deemed to be suspect. Evagrius was ordained as a lector by *Basil, Bishop of Caesarea*, who was then engaged with his friend *Gregory, Bishop of Nazianzus,* in establishing a monastic settlement for which they wrote a Rule that was to become a model for later monastic orders. Later Gregory ordained him as deacon and after enjoying spiritual friendships with Christians in Jerusalem he settled in the Egyptian desert to lead a monastic life.

Evagrius' reputation has now been rehabilitated and his influence acknowledged. His now-correctly attrib-uted *Praktikos* and *Chapters on Prayer*, which elaborate on Desert teaching, saturated subsequent monastic writ-ing, even where they are not acknowledged as sources. Today's culture emphasizes intellectual property rights, which requires acknowledgment of borrowing and cita-tion from other sources in order to avoid charges of pla-giarism: in the ancient world, by contrast, it was normal, even desirable, to build up a body of learning drawing on and incorporating the wisdom of earlier threads. The Rab-binic tradition does something similar by adding layers of interpretation to Hebrew Scriptural sources and connec-tions between existing texts; the exegesis itself then serves to inform the reader of the complete teaching. Islam has hadiths, which interpret the Qur'an. And in the New Testament we see Jesus frequently saying within his own parables and elsewhere "It is written . . . ," meaning he is referring to the Scriptures which nourished his religious life even as he developed a new understanding of what it meant to be righteous in God's eyes. And so the simple but profound insights of the *Desert Fathers* are absorbed into the subsequent tradition, often without any acknowl-edgement. Indeed, one of the main collections of Desert Wisdom is known as *The Anonymous Collection.* Absorb-ing the wisdom of previous generations honored them and showed that you were maintaining and preserving the tradition.

Evagrius' texts contain much very readable advice for monks, and are highly accessible to the modern reader as well. One of the key points he makes is that in the battle against evil thoughts and actions one must first address the *logismoi*, the underlying intentions and prompts to thoughts which if allowed to flourish will become sinful deeds. It is from his analysis of the eight evil thoughts that the medieval concept of the seven deadly sins was spawned. He lists them as gluttony, lust, avarice, sadness (in the sense of the self-pitying regret for having given up one's former life), anger, *acedia* (a compound of listlessness and despondency), vainglory, and pride.[2] He recommends as the main antidote to these corrosive desires a combina-tion of reading the Scriptures and other spiritual works, vigils, and prayer. Evagrius urges monks to:

> Pray first for the gift of tears so that by means of sorrow you may soften your native rude-ness. Then having confessed your sins to the Lord you will obtain pardon for them. Pray with tears and your request will find a hearing. Nothing so gratifies the Lord as supplication offered in the midst of tears.[3]

This may seem to contradict the injunction to work at extirpating sadness, listed as one of the problematic emotions. But the grief that prompts penitent tears is of

2. Sinkewicz, *Evagrius of Pontus*, 93.
3. Ibid., 193.

a different order to self-pitying indulgence. The "gift of tears" is a particular type of grief known as *penthos*, or joy-bearing grief; it is an example of *apatheia*. It is not a social or emotional sadness though it does convey a sense of loss. The grief of *penthos* is remorse at having (through sin) created a barrier between oneself and God. Just as a child weeps when its mother goes out of the room, because it fears it has lost her, so a truly penitent person laments the alienation from God caused by their misdeeds and those of their fellow creatures. Just as God's love for humanity does not simply equate to the carnal love between humans (even though it is often described in such symbolic terms, not least in the Song of Songs) so the penitent's desire for God is spiritualized and whilst the language of human loss and yearning may be used of both experiences, *penthos* relates to an entirely different experience. It denoted not a self-absorbed sadness but a grief for the fallenness of the world as well as one's own contribution to that. Because acknowledging such shortfallings began to erode the barrier erected by sin, *penthos* is a joyful kind of mourning. What could be more joyful than being restored to God's favor? The joy and sadness are mingled "like honey in a honeycomb," John Climacus says, in imitation of Psalm 19:9–10.[4] It is associated with remembrance of death as the ultimate "giving up" of the world and inevitable end of physical life, to which one should therefore not become attached. The reward of the life to come is greater than anything which can be enjoyed today. The benefits of *penthos* are widely attested in the Christian tradition. It is telling that Evagrius says that tears are among the first thing you should pray for; because they soften the heart they will open the way for greater repentance. By incremental steps

4. Luibheid, *Climacus*, 141.

initial penitence leads to further penitence on a pathway leading to forgiveness, restoration to God, and spiritual joy.

The Eastern Christian tradition teaches that spiritual mourning should be instinctive and wholehearted and that through it you become God-like or deified. Mourning is often described as incompatible with what monks disparagingly refer to as "theology" by which they mean abstract speculation, or a forensic attempt to rationalize what they feel should be an intuitive experience. This distinction between intuitive and intellectualized was at the heart of Symeon's argument with the learned and scholastic Stephen of Alexina, who prior to his appointment in the Byzantine court had been the area bishop for Nikomedia. The apparent conflict between formally educated and cardiac learners (people who learned by heart) was also well established in the tradition: whether it was real or merely perceived for hagiographical purposes is a moot point. Personal holiness was presented as intrinsic, simply "there" in some people, and reinforced by the pious lifestyle they adopted, rather than being acquired through complex schooling. But this is disingenuous, as the same monastic tradition insists on monks being educated by their spiritual leaders, and encourages them to access at the very least the Scriptures and often other devotional books too.

St. John Climacus

Evagrius was not the only exponent of penitent tears; John Climacus, the seventh-century Abbot of a monastery on Mount Sinai, was also extremely influential on Symeon and other monastic writers in both the East and West of the Christian world. Stethatos' biography says that Climacus' *Ladder* was one of the books that Symeon sought out from his family library to take on his state travels during the Lenten period when he was undergoing instruction from Eulabes. (The text is now read every Lent in Orthodox monasteries across the world.) His *Ladder of Divine Ascent* includes as each of the "rungs" of his meta-phorical ladder a separate step to take towards union with God. The steps or rungs deal with virtues to acquire and vices to avoid, variously schematized by modern scholars. Climacus draws on the Evagrian understanding of thought preceding action in justifying the location of Step Seven, which is entirely devoted to *penthos*. He places it after a chapter on remembrance of death and sin. The tears of true mourning for sin will help to extinguish the flames of desire, which distract the monk from focusing on God. While no one can avoid physical death, true conformity to Christ through repentance can lead to eternal life, the life of the Spirit.

Penthos is depicted by Climacus and others in the tradition as "joy-bearing grief"; it is a charism or holy gift that contains within it an apparent contradiction that in the corporeal life of human existence seems puzzling. How can grief or mourning be a happy or desirable ex-perience? How can they be combined? As we have seen above, Climacus describes the two emotions as mingled together like honey in a honeycomb: you cannot separate them from each other. He refers to a *Desert Father*, Abba Isaiah, in his explanation that through this type of spiritual mourning the penitent moves ever closer to God; mourn-ing is a "bridal garment" in which you can face God with-out fear, knowing you have prepared yourself by adorning yourself in an appropriate manner. Holy mourning is "the spiritual laughter of the soul."[5] Pricking the conscience

5. Luibheid, *Climacus*, 140.

purifies the soul and drives out pride, anger, and physical self-indulgence. At the same time, joy-bearing grief is also talked about as a physical experience: the tears shed are real physical ones; they flow down the face of the penitent. Syrian commentators talk about them even carving a groove down the cheeks because of the intensity of mourning experienced by the truly penitent. To weep so much is a sign of true enlightenment; it also enables it to continue to take place. It was his Studite mentor's own experience of weeping that was one of the factors that so convinced Symeon that Eulabes was a genuinely spiritually mature man, worthy of his discipleship.

The Studite Tradition

From the Evagrian model of awareness of sinful impulses the Studite tradition in which Symeon was trained evolved its distinctive insistence on the need for confession of even the earliest promptings towards sin. As we have seen, the *typikon* of the Studite monastery required this almost perpetual disclosure of sin, and this included the Evagrian sense of the intention behind the act. It was crucial to admit to (in modern day parlance, "to own") the intentions, daydreams, and fantasies that, left untended, could develop into actual thoughts, which in turn might cause sinful actions, which would require formal confession and sacramental absolution. That tears should accompany all stages of repentance was another Studite teaching; they should flow at the remembrance of death, at awareness of one's shortcomings, and should definitely accompany the taking of communion. In the Studite monastery Symeon was taught never to make his communion without tears, and he placed similar expectations on his monks when he became an Abbot. To this day one of the prayers Orthodox

Christians are expected to say privately before they receive communion is derived from one of Symeon's prayers, in which the penitent asked to be washed with tears.[6] This shows how important this aspect of his teaching was, and continues to be, within his religious tradition. He asserted that: "With your eyes opened by tears, you will see him whom no man has ever seen"[7] (Ps 81:12). This must be the pinnacle of Christian asceticism. The contemplative life aspired to achieve the vision of God, the invisible Godhead made visible in the incarnate Christ. Clearly Symeon's own experience of visionary encounters with God, associated with his holy father in God, predisposed him to use tears as the "gold standard" of the ascetical life. The mimetic nature of monastic life meant that in turn he would insist his monks also aspired to the conscious experience of God through penitent tears.

Symeon's Appropriation of the Earlier Tradition of Tears

Evidence from Symeon's own writings and other sources suggest that he drank deep at the well of Desert wisdom as well as being shaped by the Studite tradition. He also recalls, while not actually citing, some aspects of the more *encratic* approach of the early Syrian monastic movement, within which the teachings of Isaac of Nineveh, a contemporary of John Climacus, were dominant. These sources provided rich spiritual nourishment for an earnest young man who had enjoyed the pleasures of high life at the Byzantine court and maybe felt he had much to repent from. Symeon adds a distinctive contribution to his inheritance

6. Alfeyev, *Tradition*, 282.
7. Ps 81:12, McGuckin, *Symeon*, 62.

of earlier traditions and writings. Drawing on his experiences of ecstatic visions, which started in adolescence and were repeated throughout his life, he insists that it is while you are weeping that you are likely to see God. Humility prompts tears and when you weep "you will find the presence of the holy and adorable Spirit. . . . The God appears to him and God looks on him."[8] Frequently he employs visual imagery to explain how this "vision" of the divine can take place. In his *First Ethical Discourse* he recalls Mark 2:4, referenced earlier. When we follow monastic discipline, he says: "Indeed something is opened up in us, like a little hole in the visible roof of the heavens and the light of the world above, immaterial and spiritual, peeks around it."[9] Weeping should be a daily event—just as he needs daily bread so a monk needs regular tears to sustain him spiritually, because tears are spiritual food.[10] Here Symeon acknowledges by name the influence of Eulabes, describing how he saw penitent tears as the means to be reborn and purify the soul so that it can enter the kingdom of heaven.[11] The rebirth motif is graphically used in *Discourse 8*, where Symeon touchingly describes the instinctive response of the human infant to literally emerging into the world; metaphorically he says the human soul:

> comes out from this world as from a dark womb
> . . . into the heavenly and intellectual light, and
> as he, so to speak, peers slightly inside it he
> is at once filled with unspeakable joy. As he
> naturally thinks of [the darkness] from which
> he has been delivered he painlessly sheds tears.

8. McGuckin, *Symeon,* 80.

9. Golitzin, *Mystical* (vol. 1), 77.

10. *Discourse 4*, De Catanzaro, *Discourses*, 85.

11. *Discourse 29*, De Catanzaro, *Discourses*, 314.

A Guide to St. Symeon the New Theologian

> This is how one begins to be counted among
> Christians.[12]

As to how to achieve tears, Symeon gives very straightforward practical advice; you must use your body to achieve redemption for your whole self. He advised that you should stand to pray (as is the manner of Eastern Christians) and having said the Trisagion (Holy, Holy, Holy) and the Lord's Prayer imagine you are in a court of law, accused of your sins. In a gestalt-type process he suggests you speak to your sins, and remind them that they have condemned you to death. As you raise in prayer your hands, which have committed sins, you should examine them, and then beat your face, tearing out and pulling at your beard until you are sufficiently penitent. Having made some prostrations and recited some psalms, "God may grant that tears and compunction come on you" and you can then give thanks for this, signing "your face and your breast and your whole body with the sign of the precious Cross, before allowing yourself to rest."[13]

The joyfulness of weeping comes about because it is accompanied by the vision of God. A long section in his *Tenth Ethical Discourse* adapts the form of the Beatitudes in Matthew 5:4; not only will those who weep find joy and their tears will be turned into joy; those who have, on earth, seen God as he truly is through light-filled repentance will see him face to face in due course. "Blessed are they" he says "who see their own clothing shining as Christ, for they shall be filled hourly with joy inexpressible and shall weep tears of such astounding sweetness, perceiving that they have become themselves already sons and daughters and co-participants of the resurrection."[14] The decision to

12. *Discourse 8*, De Catanzaro, *Discourses*, 145–46.
13. *Discourse 30*, De Catanzaro, *Discourses*, 322–23.
14. Golitzin, *Mystical* (vol. 1), 167–68.

mourn for sin acts as a leveller; Symeon goes back to the
story of Adam and Eve driven, weeping, out of Eden for
their disobedience, and asserts that God's mercy would
have enabled them to remain in paradise if only they had
repented. He further explains that since that time everyone
has had the opportunity to repent and be "honoured and
glorified" by God; all can share in this glory and become
sons of God "if we imitate his confession, his repentance,
his mourning, his tears, . . . whether they are seculars or
monks."[15] Although only a minority of people will be able
to achieve real illumination of spirit, because it requires
such persistent penitence, it is not a condition that is only
open to particular categories of people (such as ordained,
monastic, secular). As recounted in the Bible, anyone who
does the will of God and denies themselves through genuine repentance can attain the vision of God. *Deification* is
the intention of all Christians.

Having established the centrality of penitent weeping in Symeon's theology, we need to look at how his
understanding of tears related to the sacraments of the
church. Symeon's esteem of the sacraments is important
because it refutes allegations that he was prone to heretical
tendencies because of his intense fervor. For Symeon, the
experience of the vision of God and the power of penitent
tears were important, not for their own sake, but because
they enabled one to be properly prepared to receive God
through the sacraments.

Tears as a Second Baptism

Because tears can be shed throughout life, from being
a baby onwards, they can act as a constant renewal of

15. *Discourse 5*, De Catanzaro, *Discourses*, 99.

baptism, keeping the soul clear from sins that were washed away in the original baptism of water. This idea that baptism was not a "once for all" fix led some people to assume that Symeon's insistence on *perpetually* washing away sin could be interpreted as him not honoring the sacrament of baptism and its power to remove sin. This is a misreading of his ideas; he valued baptism as a key sacrament but felt that a truly penitent person should continually strive to maintain the state of purity achieved through receiving the sacraments. So this was far from being a *Pelagian* disregard for grace; rather, it was a responsibility enjoined on the penitent, reflecting their gratitude at receiving grace and their determination to maintain purity through the continuance of that divine support. Symeon once again reflects the teachings of John Climacus in this; the Sinai monk wrote: "Greater than baptism itself is the fountain of tears after baptism. . . . For baptism is the washing away of evils that were in us before, but sins committed after baptism are washed away by tears."[16] Symeon builds on this insight, adding a deeper doctrinal layer to the message by invoking the Trinity. As he puts it in *Hymn 55*:

> You have given repentance as a second purification,
>> and You have set the grace of the Holy Spirit as the goal of repentance,
>> the grace we first received in baptism.
> For you have said that grace is not only by water,
> but even more by the Spirit, in the invocation of the Trinity (Matt 3:11).[17]

Repentance and the tears that accompany it add an adult perception and sense of responsibility to the initial purification granted to an infant through baptism; here are

16. Luibheid, *Climacus*, 137.
17. Griggs, *Divine Eros,* 389.

the tears shed by Peter and the "sinful woman" who have an adult comprehension of what they have done wrong. At this later stage you can make a conscious decision about your life: this awareness is a key marker of spiritual illumination as far as Symeon was concerned. The baby who cries does so instinctively; the adult who laments does so with greater consciousness of why he or she is mourning and they can make moral decisions about how they lead their life. The tears shed at birth "are expressive of the tears of this life present here in earth";[18] the fact that a baby cries as soon as it is born is proof that mourning is an essential part of the human condition, argues Symeon. Tears shed in adult life are more heavenly. The presence of the Holy Spirit in penitent tears indicates "new birth from above," which turns humans into sons and daughters of God.[19] He corroborates this by direct reference to the Gospels. An example of this is to be found in his *First Theological Chapters*, section 35, where he describes the life-changing moment of lifting up your eyes to contemplate "the nature of reality in a way [you have] never done before," causing you to tremble and weep spontaneously, although feeling no conventional sorrow. Such tears "purify him and wash him in a second baptism, that baptism Our Lord speaks about in the Gospels: 'If a man is not born of water and the Spirit, he will never enter the kingdom of heaven' (John 3:5)."[20] His *Ethical Discourses* also talk of being continually baptized by the divine fire and Spirit of God. This perpetual flow of divine grace is mirrored by continual repentance. The role of the Holy Spirit in engendering tears is emphasized throughout his writings; just as at the moment of baptism the Holy Spirit is received, so through tears there

18. De Catanzaro, *Discourses*, 314.

19. *Discourse 8*, De Catanzaro, *Discourses*, 148.

20. McGuckin, *Symeon*, 42.

is a similar *epiclesis* (sanctifying descent of the Holy Spirit). The moment at which the bread and wine of the Eucharist are transformed into the body and blood of Christ also involves an *epiclesis*. The consciousness of the indwelling Spirit of God was what conferred authority; having Christ as "an embryo" within you was a form of blessing. Without being purified of sin one could not approach the altar for communion, so preparation in the form of penitent weeping was essential if you were to participate fully in the sacramental life of the church.

Tears and the Eucharist

In similar manner, Symeon affirms the sacrament of the Eucharist by insisting that one should never receive communion without tears. He acknowledges that this was one of Eulabes' Studite teachings; to many people this suggestion caused amazement, he records, but to him this was a blessed revelation.[21] Weeping during the Eucharist is only likely to happen, he says, if you have gotten into the habit of perpetual penitent grief. This is not to say that tears were more important than receiving the bread and wine; on the contrary, it was because participating in the divine mystery was so important that it required the utmost preparation and focus. Consuming the body and blood of Christ meant you become one with him; you will be *deified*, as John's Gospel affirms: "Unless you eat the flesh of the Son of Man and drink Him blood, you have no life in you. Whoever eats My flesh and drinks My blood has eternal life and I will raise him up at the last day. . . . He who eats My flesh and drinks My blood abides in Me, and I in him" (John 6:53–56). The most appropriate preparation

21. *Discourse 4*, De Catanzaro, *Discourses*, 70.

for this holy interchange was the relinquishing of human passions, which could be encouraged by tears. Sharing in the Eucharist, properly prepared by penitence, means sharing in the sufferings of Christ such that you can experience a daily Easter.[22] Symeon's teachings on weeping at the Eucharist are significant. He insists that those who receive the Eucharist should approach it in the right manner and is even more strict about the spiritual state of those who celebrate the sacrament, taking into their hands the holy things. If they dare to do so without being properly prepared, the elements remain nothing but unconsecrated crumbs, he suggests.[23] As with the charism of forgiveness, merely being ordained did not necessarily mean you were a suitable person to transmit the sacrament; it depended on the purity of your life, demonstrated by consciously welcoming God into your heart.

The Byzantine Tradition of Disclosure of Thoughts and Confession

As discussed earlier, two forms of "confession" took place in some Byzantine monasteries. The daily disclosure of thoughts known as *exagoureusis* was not confined to Studite monasteries; it is also commanded in the foundation documents of the eleventh-century monastery at Evergetis, whose rule may be related to the pattern established by Symeon at the monastery of St. Mamas, the *typikon* of which (compiled in the twelfth century) states the founder's desire that: "the whole assembly of brothers disclose to the superior the bruises of the soul that they have suffered or the foul thoughts themselves that spring up in them as

22. *Discourse 13*, De Catanzaro, *Discourses*, 181.

23. *Hymn 58*, Griggs, *Divine Eros,* 400–401. See also Golitzin, *Mystical* (vol. 1), 142.

human beings."[24] It is not clear quite how often such disclosure took place. In very similar language to Symeon's
Hymns, Section 7 of the *Typikon of the Theotokos Evergetis*
advocates a twice daily "confession" by the monks to the
superior, who would "apply the necessary remedy to each
person."[25] The terminology of "spiritual healer" and "physician of souls" is normal within Byzantine monasticism.

Symeon's *Letter on Confession* advises his fellow
monks to: "run to the spiritual physician and, by means
of confession vomit out the poison of sin, spitting out the
venom."[26] He follows Eulabes' advice that: "Each day you
should reveal all your thoughts to your spiritual father;
and you should accept with complete confidence what he
says to you, as if it came from the mouth of God. . . . You
must confess all the secrets of your heart, all that you have
done from your infancy until this very hour, to your spiritual father or to the abbot as if to God himself, the diviner
of hearts and minds."[27] Symeon suggests this disclosure of
thoughts should take place "every hour, if possible," which
means it could not have been done to the abbot because
of the sheer volume of spiritual direction this would entail
when he also had mundane responsibilities, including the
effective stewardship of monastic resources.[28] Another
unanswered question was how the spiritual father himself
found the time he needed for his own prayers and meditation. Eulabes' *Ascetic Discourse* expresses concern that
being a confessor could be a dangerous activity; he warns
that once you start hearing confessions you risk losing the
gifts of discernment as you will be preoccupied with "the

24. Thomas and Hero, *Foundation* (vol. 3), 1014–15.
25. Gautier, *Evergetis*, 48.
26. *Letter* 1, Turner, *Epistles*, 101.
27. *The Philokalia* (vol. 4), 52–53.
28. *Discourse 26*, De Catanzaro, *Discourses*, 283.

examination of other people's thoughts." An option he recommends by way of protection against this would be to cease hearing confession and giving counsel, as an act of humility, in order to recover the gift of insight.[29]

Quite what was disclosed in these "confessions" cannot be determined. Rather than sins actually committed, the disclosure may have been of the underlying *logismoi*. Symeon describes disclosure of thoughts as: "nothing other than the necessary avowal or recognition of one's own failings and foolishness, that is, a realization of one's [spiritual]poverty."[30]

The status of such disclosure is controversial and ambiguous. It could not have been sacramental confession because of the common practice that the man hearing such disclosure was not necessarily ordained: the *typikon* of St. Mamas suggests that it was possible that the abbot himself might not necessarily be ordained, yet, "all have him as a common and spiritual father *even if perhaps he happens to be unordained* (my italics), because he has assuredly the permission from the most holy and ecumenical patriarch, having been empowered to apply also the remedy that is suitable to each illness."[31] If this was the case when the *typikon* of St. Mamas was written down in the twelfth century it must reflect practices common at the time of Symeon. Evidently there was scope to share the pastoral responsibility between the "physician" who took care of the daily disclosure of thoughts and the "father" who was the abbot: "But, if it is disagreeable to anyone . . . to have one's own father also as a physician, let him tell his father in secret his own purpose and the latter will take care to send him off to whomever the superior himself wishes or even to one of

29. *Philokalia* (vol. 4), 55–56.

30. Golitzin, *Mystical* (vol. 3), 187.

31. Thomas and Hero, *Foundation* (vol. 3), 1014.

the priests of the monastery, who is both more devout and more aged."[32]

Rather than spelling out what the different forms of confession might entail Symeon gives a series of biblical proof-texts extolling the virtues of cleansing your soul and the rewards that will follow. He uses the parable of the Good Samaritan to show how necessary it is to be helped by "a sympathetic and compassionate physician, . . . an intercessor and friend of God, someone capable of restoring him to his former state and reconciling him to God the Father."[33] Because the spiritual father was the monk's intermediary there was especial merit in confessing thoughts to him, as he could intercede for you on the Day of Judgment. The *typikon* of St. Mamas gives this advice:

> No one at all should fail to understand how much more painless it is to declare one's secret to a person, and him a shepherd who is both sympathetic and of like nature, than to be convicted in the presence of the angels and the whole race of mankind and God himself.[34]

In itself this was an accepted practice, certainly in monasteries that drew their practices from the Studite tradition. Although in this Symeon was not innovative, because of the other controversial practices to do with his high regard for Eulabes, the established church seems to have misread these guidelines as being a wholesale attack on the sacraments of ordination and remission of sins.[35] Our final chapter will explore Symeon's intellectual and spiritual legacy.

32. Thomas and Hero, *Foundation* (vol. 3), 1014.

33. Golitzin, *Mystical* (vol. 3), 191.

34. Thomas and Hero, *Foundation* (vol. 3), 1014–15.

35. Morris, *Monks and Laymen*, 94.

SIX

St. Symeon the New Theologian's Legacy

Symeon himself was acutely aware that his reputation was not positively received. In several of his texts, such as his hymns and his fourth letter, he describes himself as being reviled, condemned, or despised by a range of people; the laity, bishops, monks, and priests.[1] The reasons he gives for not being accepted in his lifetime include the criticism for his veneration of Eulabes, and his insistence that such people are understood to be living saints because they had received visions of divine light. To assert that someone could be regarded as a saint even during their life time was especially controversial. There was also the clash between his understanding of the mystical encounter as being the validation of *deification* and the ordained authority of the established church through its priests and bishops. His strong focus on the need for repentance was not innovative, but the insistence that it was demonstrated by tears was further evidence of his intense experiential approach.

1. Alfeyev, *Tradition*, 271.

In addition to these theological issues, his development of an autobiographical method of communicating his ideas was unusual and disturbing. At one and the same time he seemed to insist that *deification* was potentially open to all and, conversely, that only an elite would actually be able to achieve it as few people would devote sufficient faith and effort to renouncing the sinful ways of their past. As he puts it in *Hymn 27*:

> Do not say that God is not seen by humans.
>
> Do not say: "Human beings do not see divine light,"
>
> Or that it is impossible in the present times! . . .
>
> . . . it is very possible for those who wish it,
>
> But only for as many as life has provided with purification of the passions.[2]

His zealous reform of St. Mamas along those mystical lines clearly failed to receive an unambiguous and sustained welcome. But his teachings, as we have seen, also affirm (even insist on) the crucial contribution played to spiritual life by the sacraments of baptism and Eucharist and the central place of Holy Scripture. These are mainstream tenets of Christian teaching. In due course his reputation was rehabilitated, and in the last four or five hundred years has expanded throughout the Christian world.

It is not known quite when he was canonized, but the fact that he was shows that in due course his enormous contribution to the spiritual life of the church came to be recognized. It would be useful to know why Stethatos felt he had to wait thirty years before he started recording the life of his master; the likelihood is that this time frame also related to the delay in canonizing Symeon. One criterion for canonization is miracle-working, and Stethatos' biography records a number of striking examples of miracles,

2. *Hymn 27*, Griggs, *Divine Eros*, 208.

both during his life and afterwards. Some of these are conventional healings, but one was a bizarre punishment meted out to a visiting monk who had doubts about Symeon's holiness: he was discovered hanging in the air in front of the icon of Symeon. It was only after prolonged application of oil from the lamp that hung in front of the icon (a standard practice) that the "audacious" man was released from this posture and lowered to the ground.[3] A post-mortem appearance of Symeon to a prospective hermit named Philotheos granted him the ability to be abstinent about food.[4] Most significantly of all, Stethatos records how Symeon appeared to him in visions, commissioning him to write the biography and to edit the written works of his spiritual master. This placed Stethatos as a link in the "golden chain" of illuminated ascetics, and gave credibility to his biography of his inspiring master.

Symeon's Influence on the Hesychast Movement

The reception of Symeon's teachings was mixed. His teachings on the importance of mystical encounters found favor in the second half of the thirteenth century when Nicephoros the Hesychast attributed some of his insights in his *On Watchfulness and the Guarding of the Heart* to Symeon.[5] Other sources for this text were monks whose work Symeon was familiar with, such as Antony and John Climacus as well as the Syrian writers Marcarius and Isaac. Nicephoros was a Western monk who moved to Mount Athos to practise a life of solitude or *hesychia*. He directly quotes Symeon only once in the published edition of his text, but

3. Greenfield, *Life*, 347–53.

4. Ibid., 363–69.

5. *Philokalia* (vol. 4), 194–206.

other manuscript versions show a number of borrowings from Symeon's writings.[6] The writings resemble the *Three Methods of Prayer* falsely attributed to Symeon elsewhere in the *Philokalia*.[7] This tradition of contemplative prayer became increasingly focused on two key features: particular physical postures to be adopted when praying and a theological means of expressing human apprehension of God as distinguishing between the unknowable divine "essence" and the perceptible "energies" of God. This distinction culminated in the teachings of Saint Gregory Palamas (1296–1359), who became the most prominent member of the *hesychast* movement. This fourteenth-century Orthodox monk engaged in a number of theological debates of which the one most relevant to Symeon's legacy is this attempt to explain the transcendence of God in his relationship to humanity. Palamas claimed that the Gospels' account of the transfiguration of Jesus Christ gave his disciples a rare opportunity to see the "uncreated light" of God, the same light that Moses saw when he too ascended the Holy Mountain to encounter God. Prayer, fasting, and penitent tears were all ways by which the faithful might be granted a glimpse of God. In his visions of God Symeon did not feel the need to analyze the quality of the mystical light in which he stood while experiencing his vision. But he suggests that it was a similar light such as that which transfigured Jesus Christ on the mountain. This aspect of his teaching was developed with theological rigor by Palamas, who was born in Constantinople and followed a life of *hesychia* on the holy mountain of Athos before becoming embroiled in a theological wrangle with Barlaam the Calabrian over the issue of the essence and energies of God. Palamas maintained that the divine light that en-

6. Alfeyev, *Tradition*, 276.
7. *Philokalia* (vol. 4), 64–75.

compassed Moses when he stood before the Almighty and that flowed from Jesus during his the transfiguration, was "uncreated"; it was a manifestation of the divine "energies" of God. However, the divine "essence" of God could not be disclosed to humanity as it was transcendent. The energies of God, which take perceptible forms, allow the Christian believer to participate in God. Barlaam argued against this that such light was no more than a simple physical radiance. Gregory Palamas explained in his *Topics of Natural and Theological Sciences* that the Syrian author who wrote under the name Dionysius, the author of the *Mystical Theology* discussed earlier, had also draw a distinction between the "illuminations in the plural" (which are the energies of God) and "the divine essence, since this is single and is altogether indivisible."[8] Section 78 of his text further explains how humanity might be able to approach God given the difference between human and divine natures: "He is not nature, because he transcends every nature; He is not a being, because He transcends every being; and nor does he possess a form, because he transcends form. How, then can we draw near to God?"[9] He replies that humans can approach God through his "energy," and since all things have energy it must be only the purified energy of one who has chosen the route of virtue that allows this to happen. It is not hard to see how Symeon's emphasis on light-filled visions of God fed into such a tradition, and retrospectively he is seen as a catalyst to the medieval *hesychast* movement.

Symeon's reception in the Slavic world proved very significant. After the fall of Constantinople in 1453 to the Muslims, the Eastern Christian tradition found a new home in Russia, Serbia, and Bulgaria, and soon afterwards in Romania and Moldavia. Evidence for this can be seen

8. *Philokalia* (vol. 4), 376.
9. *Philokalia* (vol. 4), 382.

in the large numbers of manuscripts of Symeon's works in Church Slavonic held in Moscow to this day.[10] Further "links" in the *golden chain* of spiritual succession were highly influenced by Symeon's teachings on tears, deification, and living saints. St. Seraphim of Sarov (1759–1833), St. Silouan of Mount Athos (1866–1938) and his pupil, Archimandrite Sophrony (1869–1993), are all especially associated with the teachings of Symeon.[11]

Reception elsewhere was mixed. The Bollandists, who started publishing key Christian works in their *Acta Sanctorum* series in the seventeenth century, refused to publish his works on the grounds that his teaching was heretical.[12] But in Greece the revival of Athonite monasticism through the Kollyvades monks led to enthusiastic responses to his teachings. A small portion of his writings was included in the eighteenth-century anthology of Eastern Christian spiritual writings known as *The Philokalia*. This was compiled by St. Makarios of Corinth (1731–1805) and St. Nikodemos the Hagiorite (1748–1809) and first published in 1782. They were translated into English in the late twentieth century onwards. Volume 4 of this anthology contains a version of one of Symeon's homilies from his first and main collection (*Discourse 22*), together with *One Hundred and Fifty-three Practical and Theological Texts*, of which the first 118 are cribbed from Symeon, with most of the remainder being from the *Ascetic Discourse* of Eulabes. The final "sentence" is taken from the writings of Stethatos.[13] Nicetas Stethatos' *Life* was not edited until the Jesuit Irénée Hausherr worked on it in 1928, and was only translated into English in 2013. Of his four letters, the in-

10. Alfeyev, *Tradition*, 278.

11. Alfeyev, *Tradition*, 283.

12. Greenfield, *Life*, xviii, n.61.

13. *Philokalia* (vol. 4), 11–63.

fluential one on confession was not translated until 1997[14] and the remainder not until 2009.[15] New translations into English of his letters and homilies are being commissioned during the second decade of the twenty-first century.

The Title of "New" Theologian

One aspect of Symeon's reputation is the title by which he is now known, to distinguish him from Symeon Eulabes. Although the term "theologian" sometimes had derogatory connotations in the Byzantine world, that is not what is intended by its application to Symeon. Evagrius's teaching about theology had struck home for Orthodox Christians. He said: "If you are a theologian you truly pray. If you truly pray you are a theologian." In other words, being a theologian meant that you were a practitioner, not a theorist. Set against this is an alternative definition of a theologian as one who indulged in abstract speculation, deferred to book-learning and scholastic bickering about the nature of God rather than a lived, experiential approach to Divine indwelling. This type of "theology," known as scholastic, was exemplified by Stephen of Alexina (according to his detractors) and derided within the Orthodox Christian world. Absence of formal education is often a conventional attribute for which monks are praised; to be an intuitively holy and prayerful person was seen as more important a witness to God than having the ability to put forward clever arguments and sophisticated interpretations of the religious life. Where the Eastern Christian tradition uses the title of "theologian" with great reverence it is to denote a man whose writings stem from deep mystical union

14. Golitzin, *Mystical* (vol. 3), 185–204.

15. Turner, *Epistles*.

with God. Prior to Symeon, only John the Evangelist and Apostle and the Cappadocian Father *Gregory, Bishop of Nazianzus*, had been accorded the title "theologian." Symeon would have been the first to insist that theological theorizing divorced from deep-seated belief and Christian experience made a mockery of the concept of speaking about God. Byzantine theology and the culture from which it grew were rooted in tradition, hence the complicated rituals imposed upon the Byzantine emperor in his daily worship in the court at Constantinople. In asserting the primacy of the "basics" of Christian faith (repentance, the sacraments, prayerful engagement with God) Symeon was a conservative rather than an innovative teacher. Tradition (the Greek word is *paradosis*) was a key feature in their thinking; the passing on from one generation to another of rituals, practices, and shared understandings was at the heart of Byzantine life. Just as Matthew's Gospels starts with the genealogy of Jesus, proving his kingly and priestly antecedents, so the Eastern Christian world felt the need to prove cultural lineage. For this reason, when the time came for the divine-human figure of the emperor to be born, the empresses had to give birth in a room whose walls were clad in purple marble so that her heirs could bear the title "porphyrogenetos," meaning "born in the purple chamber." Adhering to the traditions and practices of the past is fundamental to the Eastern Christian Church to this day. In October 2013, I was privileged to be present at a Liturgy at which Metropolitan Hilarion Alfeyev was presiding, in his church in Moscow. Many aspects of the service, including the semiotic use of different robes and postures, would have been recognized by Christian worshippers from a millennium ago. Unlike the Western church with its many liturgical revisions the Eastern Church holds true to very ancient practices: in Russia, the liturgy today takes place in the ancient liturgical language of Church Slavonic rather than modern Russian. So the descriptor "New" is problematic within the tradition. Applied to Symeon, it may have originally been part of a mischievous attempt to further undermine his standing immediately after his passing. It may be that the word was used to distinguish him from his father whose Christian name was the same as his adopted name. Symeon shares certain qualities with his fellow "theologians." Like Gregory Nazianzus, Symeon was more than capable of couching his theology in dramatic and effective poetry. Like John, he wrote from his own experience of the living God, and his teachings bore out the experiential nature of his faith, echoing what is recorded by the evangelist at the close of the Fourth Gospel: "This is the disciple who testifies of these things, and wrote these things; and we know that his testimony is true" (John 21:24).

Both the previous "theologians" were striking in their awareness of the importance of the inner spiritual life. In the case of Symeon it is this understanding of "theology" that pertains and not an abstract academic one derived from scholastic enquiry. Even in his insistence on the "evidence" of the vision of God and the importance of conscious acceptance of grace within the heart as sources of authentic spiritual authority, Symeon is a traditionalist rather than an innovator. Be that as it may, as with many prophetic voices, his was fated to be neglected and unheard for centuries. Perhaps some aspects of his teaching touched a nerve in clerics who were "going through the motions" of the spiritual life rather than really grappling with it; undoubtedly there were social affiliations within Byzantine society that favored both parties in the debate and probably jealousies and influences brought to bear by patrons, such as the *charistikaria* who provided financial support for monasteries.

Symeon's Teachings on Spiritual Direction

Symeon's focus on spiritual fatherhood has been especially valued in recent days. As we have noted, some of his writings were included in *The Philokalia* and this text has remained an important source of spiritual insight for Orthodox Christians. As new translations of his entire works have become available these too have been welcomed as spiritual inspiration. His insistence that good spiritual direction was what helped you to grow into a mature Christian found acceptance in modern Orthodox monasteries and parishes, where in the Western world at least one of the main functions of monasteries is to be a place to turn to for advice and counsel.[16] In modern America and northern Europe (and perhaps to a lesser extent in new accession European nations) the interplay of secular and religious life in society brings its own challenges to the process of spiritual direction. Choosing to leave behind a birth family in order to form allegiance to a new "family" of monastic brothers and sisters is readily misunderstood as joining a cult of religious extremists. The Orthodox Church is found in many countries, but unlike Roman Catholicism or the Anglican (Episcopalian) denominations its leadership is autocephalous; in other words, peculiar to that country, rather than being led from afar by one overall head, such as the Pope who from the Vatican in Rome pronounces on Roman Catholic teaching for the entire world. So there is scope for friction with different parliamentary systems as well as varying cultural expectations in a postmodern

16. Chryssavgis, *Soul Mending*, 94.

context where diversity is the norm. There are also the insights of contemporary psychotherapy to bear in mind; some people feel that the wide range of "talking therapies" now available have largely replaced the need for a spiritual advisor of the traditional sort. Just as in ancient times the authentic nature of spiritual fatherhood depends on true discernment, both of the father himself (that he is not being led astray by arrogant desires for self-aggrandizement) and of the nascent Christian who turns to him or her (in the case of a spiritual mother) that they have chosen their spiritual guide on the basis of their holiness and ability to counsel and not because they were popular in any more secular sense. Issues of what psychotherapists would call transference and countertransference may appear to arise. A particularly sad example of where spiritual direction in the modern world went very wrong was a young man known as Niko who took spiritual advice from an elder at the Greek Orthodox monastery of St. Antony, in the Sonoran Desert of Arizona. Like Symeon, this young man's family were reluctant to "lose" him from his home and they employed various modern media such as public broadcasting to highlight their unhappiness at what they felt was a cult-like adherence to his spiritual father. Like Saint Augustine, the young man had several companions who shared in his journey from the "world" to the monastery. He cited patristic writers, such as John Climacus, one of Symeon's influences, as being inspirational to him on his path towards better self-understanding and leading a godly life. Sadly the young man was unable to resolve the conflict he was experiencing between the calls of the world and the expectations of his spiritual father, and he took his own life.[17]

17. Hunt, *Uses*, 210.

In a very different context there have been issues about spiritual direction that touch on the sensitive issue of the relationship between church and state in contemporary Russia. In early 2013 a British public broadcasting station aired an interview between Steve Rosenberg, a correspondent for the British Broadcasting Corporation in Moscow, and Metropolitan Hilarion Alfeyev, who in addition to his senior clerical role in the Russian Orthodox Church is a scholar of St. Symeon the New Theologian.[18] Questions had been asked about the Russian Orthodox Church's apparent support for President Vladimir Putin, whose hold on office had begun to be described as "miraculous." It was speculated that there was a blurring between the secular and religious sources of authority here. Alfeyev insisted that a principle of mutual non-interference between church and state was adhered to. He stated that the state was unable to influence the choice of patriarch and bishop and furthermore the church could not be involved in politics, not least because clergy were not permitted to be members of political parties. Alfeyev insisted that Putin's continued political success derived from the support of ordinary Russian citizens from a number of different churches, not just the Russian Orthodox Church, who met with Putin during the election campaign. There was no official endorsement by the Russian Orthodox Church per se. Probed by Rosenberg (who noted how very differently election campaigns would run in the United Kingdom) Alfeyev conceded that different countries do things in different ways. Support for Putin depended on his own actions, he asserted, as the "social doctrine of the Russian Orthodox Church will not condone actions contrary to Christian morality and in such instances will call for civil disobedience."

18. Radio 4 Today Programme, 17 January 2013.

St. Symeon the New Theologian's Legacy

Interest in this topic has continued, however. Further discussion of President Putin's religious life was published in the *Financial Times*, an upmarket UK paper, in the weekend review edition of 26–27th January 2013.[19] Here it was the relationship between President Putin and Father Tikhon Shevkunov that was being examined. Father Tikhon is the Archimandrite of the Sretensky Monastery, Moscow. He accompanies Putin on both foreign and domestic trips, perhaps rather as St. Photius of Thessaloniki did Basil II on his military campaigns, or maybe acting a little bit as the *synkellos* Stephen did. The question was raised as to whether or not Fr. Shevkunov was Putin's *dukhovnik* or godfather, and if so whether there was some abuse of power or undue influence taking place. These recent journalistic articles show how controversial matters of faith can be, especially when attached to political leaders. In a predominantly secular society, a prominent member of the public seeking spiritual advice from a priest attracts attention. A fictional example is an episode of the popular political drama *West Wing* in which the (Roman Catholic) president makes his confession at the time that he permits an execution to take place.

In the Byzantine world spiritual guidance for all who sought it was normative. The controversy arose over whether authority over spiritual matters such as the remitting of sins lay with the established church (validated by imperial support in a mutually beneficial manner) or with those who relied on a more personal conviction of holiness due to visions of God. For Symeon it was clear that only such a direct encounter with the transcendent God empowered an ascetic, regardless of whether the church had acknowledged his holiness through ordination. In the

19. Charles Clover, "Putin and the Monk," *Financial Times*, 26/27 January 2013, 21–25.

modern world there is both suspicion about claims to holiness and great hunger for guidance and leadership, as men and women pick a path through the moral minefield of contemporary society. For some, whether in the monastery or "living in the world," the insights of Saint Symeon the New Theologian, his fervor, his dramatic use of language, and his frank disclosure of his own experiences of God, may offer some sense of direction.

Glossary of Words, Persons, and Theological Terms

Please note these terms might have a slightly different nuance in other contexts; the definitions given here are designed to enhance your understanding of the mid-Byzantine Eastern Christian context explored in this book. Unless otherwise denoted the terms are Greek.

Acedie: One of Evagrios' *logismoi*, this term denotes listlessness, lack of focus, spiritual laziness.

Agape: Christian term for love, loving kindness. It is also the word used for the Eucharist in the earliest days of the church.

Amor: Latin word for love, usually indicating sexual or romantic love.

Anathema: A term of condemnation for those who did not conform to the canons of Ecumenical Councils. It was not uncommon for certain bishops to *anathematize* (verb) fellow prelates who disagreed with them, and their followers would also be condemned.

Apatheia: A key monastic quality—the absence of passions or desire for things of the world.

Glossary of Words, Persons, and Theological Terms

Apophatic (adjective), *apophasis* (noun): The "negative way" (*via negativa*), which insists that humanity can only describe God by what is NOT known or perceived—e.g., God is *in*visible, *in*tangible, *in*finite—and that truly understanding God is something that happens beyond the limits of human language.

Apophthegmata: The brief sentences or narrative texts recorded by or from the *Desert Fathers*, giving spiritual insights and accounts of holiness among the ascetics.

Ascetic (noun/adjective): The quality of a life focused on prayer and contemplation, with the minimum of human comforts such as food, sleep, physical contact with others.

Basil, Bishop of Caesarea (330–79), known as "Basil the Great": Key member of the Cappadocian Fathers and instigator of a monastic community at Annesoi, for which he wrote a Rule that inspired subsequent monastic *typika*.

Bogomils: A neo-*Manichean* sect that developed in tenth-century Bulgaria (a place much ravaged by Basil II). It was elitist and anti-materialist. *Mani* was a third-century religious leader who taught an extreme form of dualism (the physical world being denigrated and only spiritual life being seen as valid).

Byzantine: Adjective describing both a period (the Empire which fell to the Turks in 1492) and a perspective, that of the Eastern rather than Western Christian church.

Caritas: Latin word for love, usually translated as charity.

Glossary of Words, Persons, and Theological Terms

Catechesis: A systematic means of teaching religion to initiates. In the case of Symeon, this took place through his homilies so in this context *catechesis* (plural *catecheses*) denotes the written texts of homilies or sermons he preached to his monks.

Charistikarion (noun, plural *charistikaria*): A patron in the Byzantine world; the practice whereby secular benefactors were involved in some aspects of the administration and governance of monasteries.

Deification: The exaltation of the human person to kinship with God. In Greek this is known as *theosis.*

Desert Fathers: Collective term for a number of often-anonymous monks and hermits who lived in the deserts of Egypt, Syria, or Palestine predominantly, starting in the third century. The term is commonly applied to their sayings, which were written down and disseminated later.

Dilectio: Latin word for love in the sense of taking a delight or pleasure in something or someone.

Discernment: A key monastic benchmark, the critical ability to distinguish what is God's will and to avoid being deluded by inappropriate matters.

Discourse: Another word used to denote written *homilies* or *catecheses.*

Dual natures of Christ: The doctrine that Christ was fully human and fully divine and that these two natures were indivisibly joined together in the one person of Jesus.

Glossary of Words, Persons, and Theological Terms

Economia: Literally household management, in theological contexts this refers to the compassion of God in accommodating human weakness, and the outworking of this by clergy.

Ecumenical Councils: A series of gatherings of church officials and leaders held at intervals from 325 (The Council of Nicaea) onwards to determine church doctrine and to deal with those who did not conform to such doctrine.

Encratic: Adjective describing extreme asceticism, often in Syrian religious contexts.

Epiclesis: The sanctifying descent of the Holy Spirit to earth, during the sacraments or other key religious moments.

Essence and Energies of God: Eastern Christianity distinguishes between the "essence" of God as His ontological Divine Nature (the Greek word is *ousia*) and the "energies" as the means by which this divine nature are communicated actively to humanity. Both are eternal and uncreated.

Exagoureusis: Disclosure of thoughts, sometimes seen as a form of confession, but not having the same sacramental force of confession to a priest.

Golden Chain: Concept originally from Middle Platonism; an allegorical explanation for how Zeus connected the world to the sun by a rope or pulley. The Christian writer Iamblichus adapted it to denote the way in which successive generations of holy people inspire each other.

Glossary of Words, Persons, and Theological Terms

Gregory, Bishop of Nazianzus (329–89): One of the highly influential Cappadocian Fathers. Like Symeon he wrote in a very wide range of styles and genres, including theological discourses, exegesis, and poetry.

Gregory, Bishop of Nyssa (331–95): Close friend of Gregory Nazianzus and younger brother of Basil the Great. Wrote spiritual texts and supported the cause of Christological orthodoxy.

Hagiography (adj. *hagiographic*): Literally, writing about holiness, the term is applied to a style of writing that seeks to praise the subject in a biased manner, emphasizing their good qualities.

Heterodox: A position that varies from the *orthodox* or correct doctrine. A less derogatory term than "heretic," implying divergence of belief rather than doctrinal error.

Hesychastic: From the Greek work *hesychia*, meaning "stillness," "centeredness"; the term refers to the religious movement that promoted contemplative prayer when withdrawn from "the world".

Homily: Another word for a sermon; in our context implying the written form of sermons often known also as *discourse* or *catechesis*.

Idiorrhythmic (or *idiorhythmic*): Literally, following one's own devices. Adjective describing monasteries that run according to their own rules.

John Climacus (575–650): Monk from Sinai whose spiritually uplifting text *The Ladder of Divine Ascent* was, and continues to be, widely read in Eastern Christian circles.

John of the Cross (1542–91): Spanish mystic and Carmelite monk who described his experience of God as arising from a "dark night of the soul"; often seen as contributing to the *via negativa* or apophatic tradition.

Kontakion (plural *kontakia*): Hymns and other service material written to commemorate the faithful departed.

Logismos (plural *logismoi*): The evil propensities that precede thought and wrong-doing, according to Evagrius. These were developed into the concept of the Seven Deadly Sins.

Mendicant: Those within religious orders who live by begging or living providentially, allowing God to provide for their needs, rather than following a fixed means of earning a living.

Menologion: An office book including a list of saints and the days on which they are to be commemorated by the church. Basil's *Menologion* was an illustrated calendar of saints' days, lavishly decorated. The manuscript *Vaticanus graecus* (1613) is in the Vatican library.

Messalians: Sect who focused on prayer, believing that prayer alone was sufficient to ensure salvation. The name comes from a corruption of the Syriac word for prayer. Evidence about their actual existence rather than their reputation is sketchy.

Metropolitan (Bishop): The key bishops in a city or metropolitan area, such as Constantinople or Nikomedia.

Glossary of Words, Persons, and Theological Terms

Orthros: The early morning monastic service of prayer and praise also known as *matins.*

Paradosis: The Orthodox Christian concept of tradition as a marker of true teaching; the stable transmission of ideas from one generation to another was highly valued.

Parakoimomenos: Literally the one who sleeps next to the Emperor, a trusted official within the Byzantine Civil Service.

Patriarch, Patriarchate: The bishop and his administration/official residence.

Pelagius (adj. *Pelagian*) (350–425): British ascetic who argued with Augustine of Hippo about the concept of grace in Christian life. Pelagius claimed it was not necessary to have divine grace in order to please God. This was deemed heretical as it was in conflict with Augustine's teaching about original sin and the necessity of grace.

Penthos: Translated as "joy-bearing grief," this denotes the penitential weeping that, paradoxically, was full of grace because by acknowledging sinfulness one grew closer to reconciliation to God.

Perichoresis: The intermingling (inter-penetration) of the divine three persons of the Trinity, Father, Son, and Holy Spirit, denoting their indivisibility.

Philanthropia: Love for fellow humans, usually translated as philanthropy.

Philokalia: "Love of the beautiful" or "what is good"; refers to an anthology of writings on the spiritual life from around thirty-six authors, compiled in 1782. After the Bible, it is the single text most widely read by Orthodox Christians.

Stephen of Alexina: Former Metropolitan Bishop of Nikomedia, he was the trusted *synkellos* to Basil II and held an important position within the Byzantine church at this time.

Summa: The culmination of a person's religious thoughts and teachings; their key witness to what they believed.

Synkellos: A private advisor to the Patriarch, literally one who inhabited his "cell" or chambers with him. This role involved considerable political acumen.

Synod: The so-called "endemousa synodos" was the "standing" committee of bishops who conducted the business of the *Patriarchate*. It included a number of key office holders or functionaries.

Theophany: A visible manifestation of God granted to human beings.

Typikon (plural *typika*): The rule book devised by each monastery. They frequently cited the *typika* of earlier or similar monasteries.

Vita: A written biography, or literally "life story," of a celebrated figure. Because of the context they were frequently *hagiographical,* in other words, designed to focus on the special virtues of the subject, rather than being an objective account.

Bibliography

Primary Sources

De Catanzaro, Carmino J., trans. *Symeon the New Theologian: The Discourses*. New York: Paulist, 1980.

Golitin, Alexander., trans. *St Symeon The New Theologian: On the Mystical Life: The Ethical Discourses*. 3 vols. Crestwood, NY: St. Vladimir's Seminary Press, 1995–97.

Greenfield, Richard P. H., trans. *Stethatos Niketas: The Life of Saint Symeon the New Theologian*. Cambridge, MA: Dumbarton Oaks Medieval Library, 2013.

Griggs, Daniel, trans. *Divine Eros: Hymns of Saint Symeon the New Theologian*. Crestwood, NY: St. Vladimir's Seminary Press, 2010.

Hausherr, Iréné, and Gabriel Horn, trans. "Nicetas Stethatos: Vie de Syméon le Nouveau Théologien." In *Un Grand Mystique byzantine: Vie de Syméon le Nouveau Théologien par Nicétas Stethatos*, lvi–lxvii. Rome: Orientalia Christiana XII (45), 1928.

Luibheid, Colm, and Norman Russell, trans. *John Climacus: The Ladder of Divine Ascent*. New York: Paulist, 1982.

Luibheid, Colm, trans. *Pseudo-Dionysius: The Complete Works*. London: SPCK, 1987.

McGuckin, Paul, trans. *Symeon the New Theologian: The Practical and Theological Chapters and the Three Theological Discourses*. Kalamazoo, MI: Cistercian, 1982.

Palmer, G. E. H., et al., trans. *The Philokalia: The Complete Text*, vol. 1. London: Faber and Faber, 1979.

Bibliography

————, trans. *The Philokalia: The Complete Text*, vol. 4. London: Faber and Faber, 1995.

Puech, Henri-Charles, and André Valliant, eds. *Comas the Priest: Le Traité contre les Bogomiles de Cosmas le Prêtre*. Paris: Imprimerie Nationale, 1945.

Robertson, A., trans. *Athanasius' Life of Antony*. In Nicene and Post-Nicene fathers, Second Series, vol. 4, edited by Philip Schaff, 188–221. Reprint. Peabody, MA: Hendrickson, 1995.

Sewter, E. R. A., trans. *Michael Psellos: Fourteen Byzantine Rulers*. London: Penguin, 1953. Online: http:// www.fordham.edu/halsall/basis/psellus-chron001.asp.

Sinkewicz, R. E., trans. *Evagrius of Pontus: The Greek Ascetic Corpus*. Oxford: Oxford University Press, 2003.

Thomas, John, and Angela C. Hero, trans. *Byzantine Monastic Foundation Documents*. 5 vols. Washington, DC: Dumbarton Oaks, 2000.

Turner, H. John M., trans. *Epistles of St. Symeon the New Theologian*. Oxford: Oxford University Press, 2009.

Wortley, J., trans. *John Skylitzes: A Synopsis of Byzantine History, 811–1057*. Cambridge: Cambridge University Press, 2010.

Secondary Sources

Alfeyev, Hilarion. *St. Symeon the New Theologian and Orthodox Tradition*. Oxford: Oxford University Press, 2000.

Charanis, Peter. "The Monk as an Element of Byzantine Society." *Dumbarton Oaks Papers* 25 (1971) 61–84.

Chryssavgis, John. *Soul Mending: The Art of Spiritual Direction*. Brookline, MA: Holy Cross Orthodox Press, 2000.

Gautier, Paul. "Le typikon de la Thétokos Evergeteis." *Revue des Etudes Byzantines* 40 (1982) 5–101.

Holmes, Catherine. *Basil II and the Governance of Empire 976–1025*. Cambridge: Cambridge University Press, 2005.

Hunt, Hannah. *Clothed in the Body: Asceticism, the Body and the Spiritual in the Late Antique Era*. Farnham, UK: Ashgate, 2012.

————. *Joy-bearing Grief: Tears of Contrition in the Writings of the Early Syrian and Byzantine Fathers*. Leiden: Brill, 2004.

————. "The Reforming Abbot and His Tears: *Penthos* in Late Byzantium." In *Spirituality in Late Byzantium*, edited by Eugenia Russell, 13–20. Cambridge: Cambridge Scholars Publishing, 2009.

————. "Uses and Abuses of Spiritual Authority in the Writings of St. Symeon the New Theologian." In *The Philokalia: A Classic Text of Orthodox Spirituality*, edited by Brock Bingaman and Bradley Nassif, 203–15. Oxford: Oxford University Press, 2012.

Hussey, Joan. "Byzantine Monasticism." In *Cambridge Medieval History,* vol. IV, Part 2, 161–84 and 439–43. 2nd ed. Cambridge: Cambridge University Press, 1966.

Krausmüller, Dirk. "Religious Instruction for Laypeople in Byzantium: Stephen of Nicomedia, Nicephorus Ouranos, and the Pseudo-Athanasian *Syntagma ad Quendam Politicum.*" *Byzantion* 77 (2007) 239–50.

McGinn, Bernard. "Mysticism." In *The New Westminster Dictionary of Christian Spirituality*, edited by Philip Sheldrake, 19–25. Louisville: Westminster John Knox, 2005.

McGuckin, John A. "The Church: Monasticism and Monasteries." In *The Oxford Handbook of Byzantine Studies*, edited by Elizabeth Jeffreys, 611–20. Oxford: Oxford University Press, 2008.

Morris, Rosemary. *Monks and Laymen in Byzantium, 843–1118.* Cambridge: Cambridge University Press, 1995.

Treadgold, Warren. *A History of the Byzantine State and Society.* Stanford: Stanford University Press, 1997.

Index

Index

Index

Made in the USA
Columbia, SC
19 December 2018